MY LAST DUNGAREES

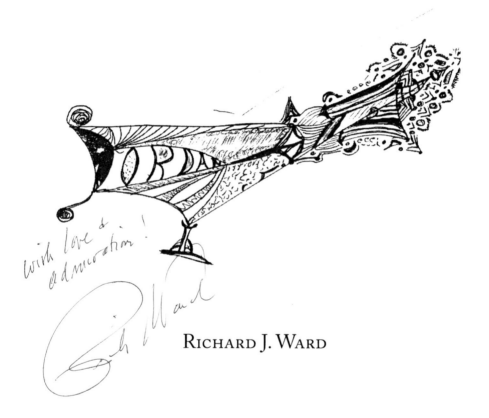

with love &
admiration!

RICHARD J. WARD

authorHOUSE®

AuthorHouse™
1663 Liberty Drive
Bloomington, IN 47403
www.authorhouse.com
Phone: 1-800-839-8640

ISBN: 978-1-4389-7553-5 (sc)
ISBN: 978-1-4389-7554-2 (hc)

Printed in the United States of America
Bloomington, Indiana
This book is printed on acid-free paper.

Contents

CHAPTER 1

Dungarees, Doodles and Right-Side Brain Gurus

Suddenly, lots of time on your hands. The predictable nine- to-five schedule— gone. The engrossing work load that consumes so much of mind and energy—gone. The daily personal interaction with colleagues, clients, students, the complexities of institutional management and finance, whatever—gone. At least a slight sense of panic prevails early on. Women handle this vacuity better than men, this much I know.

All these and more ponderings can be woven into an opening orientation of your life story as it also very soon helps greatly to take up the slack in available retirement time. Fixing up the odds and ends of your own and your wife's "to do" list— the loose shelf board, cleaning up the mess in the basement, painting the bad spots on the porch banister, the list is endless—most of it can be done when you need a break from sitting and writing. You have to spend time jostling the memory, setting up your life-story outline and recording detail that fills out the outline. You seek and find stories and anecdotes about your past exploits, pull out the scrapbook clippings, write up and enthuse about the comedic but wonderful chums you nearly got killed with in those reckless episodes you couldn't tell your parents about at the time. Also, there are always the favorite sports you excelled at among your peers, accompanied by the supporting columns in the saved local gazette. All this pulling together of stuff takes much sitting down and massaging of the material. Once committed to this process it becomes a personal challenge and, believe it or not, it becomes a lot of fun.

Then you go about finding a skein or thread or symbol that in your mind represents a link to your life story, and even your outlook on life itself. In my own case, the skein or symbol was a pair of dungarees, derived from my struggle to find constructive activity in retirement that would put my *full* mind to work. By full mind I mean that my profession as an economist demanded full use of that more objective and analytical brain on the left side of my head. It was in the art world that I would find an outlet for putting the more artistic and subjective right brain to work—not just in my hobbies and artistic expression per se, but also in how I wrote.

And in the art world many artists wear jeans or dungarees. Economists, especially those who become Deans, don't wear jeans or dungarees to work. And yes, though new to me, there's a difference between the two, as is probably well known by others. So I took myself to a national chain store to inquire into and buy the denims artists wear.

Now, getting to the origin of this name 'dungaree.' Give some credit to the Indians— of India, that is. They came up with the name, yes, but now both the name and the making of the product are well nigh universal. The "dungaree" is, in effect, everywhere, both in use and in production! It was said to be associated in name with a Hindu goddess who lived on a Dungar, a hill or small mountain. The Goddess had nothing to do with the fabric that became so famous, only that she was connected to the place. The dungaree fabric was produced in a place called Dongari Killa, which was also called Fort George. As a defense against enemies, ideal locations for forts— as every proper British military man knew— are typically on a hill. This one happens to be Mumbai, once called Bombay, India. There, the factories made and sold a coarse, poorly-woven calico and sold it mostly to the poorest people. The market for the product gradually spread, taking the name of dungaree wherever it went. Naturally, eventually other countries and companies got into the thriving business; only the fabric used became denim— a tough, double-threaded (twilled, they called it), cotton cloth, originating—intriguingly — in the city of Nimes in Southeastern France.

Oddly enough too, Nimes also figures in the reputed origin of the name "jeans," since the denim bluish fabric was also shipped to Genoa, Italy, where it was called bleu de genes (the French for Genoa), hence "blue jeans."

The jeans and dungarees we know and wear and stylize today have to meet the sophisticated and sometimes crazy whims of every male and female in the modern world. Even "shortalls" and "skirtalls" for the bold and saucy have become popular as cool summer wear. In the breakdown of formality that has spread like a rash through many respectable and demanding professions around us, casual wear has become almost the norm. Many Microsoft professionals from the highest rank on down go to work in denim jeans. The entire computer and high tech world has signed on to the liberated atmosphere of the smart Jean look in the office. Teachers at all levels of education now show up in jeans, some of them touting patches to demonstrate how "with it" they are with the kids they teach. How far has the coarse, poorly- woven cloth strayed and prospered from its humble makings in the world of poverty that was Dongari Killa!

There is a clear difference between the jean and the dungaree, though they are both made traditionally of the same fabric. The jean, the plain, stylistic, tight-fitting statement of chic and "with it"; the dungaree, the working jean, with loops to hold tools, added pockets for artifacts of the carpenter or other trades.

I have to tell you now how I made my way from a fairly conservative academic administrator who long ago gave up the overalls for the grey suit and tie, and now in my 80's found myself compelled to plunge into the denim jean and dungaree racks. It had to do with my new status on the Board of Directors of Art Gallery X in the city of New Bedford, Massachusetts. In the beginning, it was a fuzzy venture into the unknown and into what my prejudices led me to think was the disassembling, free-spirited world of the artist.

This artist's journey began with an impulsive habit, like a tic, that got me into doodling. The habit really blossomed during graduate school days. Either boredom invaded my concentration, shutting down the drone from the podium, or I had half-way through the class grasped the message. When either of these happened, my right arm and the pen between my fingers started moving up the page, seeking creative expression and outlet for the abstractions that lingered in that "arty" right side of the brain. Strange creatures, symmetric structures, futuristic space ships, one labeled "Guru" in fancy robes— sun rays shooting up from his head and a long left arm extended into a shark's head and toothy mouth. Another is called a "Beach Creature with Built-in Geiger Counter." Well over one hundred of these abstract renditions emerged spontaneously from my pen into formations, every one of them different in some respect. Think of our dual-hemisphere brains whose subjective images and expressions of patterns in art or music lie dormant in that right brain of so many people, never to be seen or heard. Retirement offers a terrific opportunity to rouse that sleeping potential from its torpor.

To focus on a career preparation as an economist, a doctor, an engineer or a CEO of a corporation, the subjective right brain must find relief in hobbies: play the piano, visit the Louvre, the British Museum, or like Churchill take up the brushes and paint scenes of the surrounding glory from the vista of your back yard or on banks of a river. I have known doctors and engineers who relieve these right-brain frustrations by rebuilding antique cars, and they do it with superb patience and skill. Some famous creations are produced from these hobbies; you've seen them on television documentaries depicting elegant architectural structures, music, paintings.

Little did I know that my compulsive hobby would lead me ultimately toward a better appreciation of spirituality—nor that it would lead me, archly enough, into this dungaree world.

The compulsive doodling I speak of endured into graduate schooling in the 50's, right through my doctoral preparation, then persisted at long-winded professional conventions during my teaching and sojourns in business and government. Doodles became part of my abstract being, even as I had to focus on the essential daily pragmatics before me in order to succeed in a career as an economist. These doodles just showed up, always from the same ink pen I happened to be taking notes with. Notebook, stationery, official letter-head sheets, printed agendas handed out in professional meetings, telephone pads or paper scraps by the phone, hotel stationery or pads, lined or otherwise— each and all wound up with one of the strange and yet often appealing designs. Sometimes, the paper I doodled on had little room for anything else but its intended message. But, somehow, I would squeeze and contrive a doodle on the top, the sides, or the bottom. By some happenstance I can't explain—because it was instinctive rather than planned— I would eventually retain these doodles and later, when the content of notes taken, or papers or documents written were no longer needed, the doodles were torn from the pages and stuffed into a file cabinet under D. By the time I became conscious of what you'd call a collection, almost thirty years had gone by—yes, I said *thirty years*! — I had about one hundred and fifty doodles in two files!

Question: what to do with doodles? First, I have to improve your understanding about these doodles. They were not just kid's stuff; they were elaborate and complicated, each different and interesting, especially— I thought then— from a psychologist's view of the world and our place in it. Twenty years before I retired I decided to ask a specialist in the art world to have a look at them, tell me what to do with them, hopefully avoiding obscenities. The specialist had connections, was a consultant to the publication design office of one of America's most distinguished universities, as well as an artist of note in his own right. He sent selections of my doodles to the experts at that institution. I waited with some concern about exposing myself to ridicule or even, worse, psychoanalysis.

My art specialist received two letters from colleagues and included his own. They bowled me over. Two of the letters are a page long, the third one three pages. Here are excerpts:

"Your doodles are certainly fascinating ….indeed, many are works of art. They certainly make interesting viewing and they deserve publication somewhere." - Thomas B. Blodgett, Senior Editor, *Harvard Business Review*

5

"I would like to use your doodles in my class as a learning tool and an excellent teaching aid for students.....I found them fresh, spontaneous, fascinating and meaningful...They are intricate patterns and symbols that touch on humor, frustrations, magic, invention, religion and abstract designs." -Lisa Collins, Professor of Visual Symbols and Senior Editorial Consultant, Harvard University

"Doodling is a magical, mind-opening diagramming process for analyzing all kinds of phenomena...These drawings...revealed or at least suggested a rich world of thought and fantasy....The drawings of Saul Steinberg, a contributing humorist to the *New Yorker* come to mind, which carry his social commentary about the immediate and extended worlds around him." --Dietmar Winkler, Dean of Visual and Performing Arts and Professor Emeritus, University of Massachusetts; former senior consultant, Harvard publications.

These letters took me completely by surprise. I felt tingles up the spine and fear in my mind.

Why wasn't I overjoyed with these responses? It came to me like a revelation: If I prepare these doodles for public display, say, in art shows and appropriate museums, my professional colleagues and countless friends will conclude that this is what I have been doing all these years— on my jobs, at conferences I was paid to attend, in meetings dealing with weighty agendas. I had been doodling! This is more likely to be a problem because the doodling talent had nothing whatever to do with my work as an academic administrator and an economist.

As I absorbed the essence of this awakening, I realized I was not about to launch a career in the art world, only to cast eerie shadows over the content of my past work and career. I put the doodles back in my files until I retired. What you decide to do in retirement, whatever your specialization in your working life, it's o.k. Run with your hobbies, whatever. It was a long wait, but I was too busy to feel I had sacrificed something. The years went by fast. I proceeded to locate skilled matting and framing experts in my village and worked up my collection into a respectable-looking show for an appropriate local museum or gallery. Not being familiar with the art world, I used artist friends to contact Gallery X by phone where a supportive woman arranged for me to have a showing of my work before the Board of Directors.

Quite a change from circles I moved about in, professionally and socially. Artists are a different breed, and I wondered how I would be greeted. I climbed the steps, the bag of framed doodles under my arm, into the converted Bethel A.M.E. Church hall. Eleven people sat around the table, watching my approach. They would review my doodle renditions after the meeting. This contrast between my more conservative attire and theirs would become drastically notable later during the so-called "hanging" of one's art works.

As for the meeting, every member of that board of artists contributed to discussions and debates about programs, the budget and its adequacy or lack of it, then zeroed in on the proposed content of the next gallery show for the public. Coming from my business orientation, I was surprised and impressed with their pragmatism and attention to fiscal detail.

Meeting over, the focus turned on me. I was asked to spread my framed works out before the members, and then leave the hall while they discussed my work and whether it qualified for entry into their next show. In about fifteen minutes, I was called in and congratulated; my framed doodles passed the test. To my surprise, I was also voted in as a member of the Board. I assume they saw potential for fund-raising in my economics background. I was told that the "The Hanging" of my artwork would take place in a week from that date, starting at 7 pm.

Already, I had recognized that I had to do something about my dress code. On the night of "The Hanging," my new-found cohort of friends in the art world showed up in jeans and dungarees, holes in the knees, designer patches here and there. Some were barefoot. I was being initiated into a brave new world, and also taken back in memory to those early years when the word "jean" was not yet in use and overalls and dungarees served a working family's survival purpose. In the old days, holes and patches would have announced an embarrassing admission of poverty. Today, it is chic and stylish;

beyond this, it was, in a sense, an emblem of some transformation going on in me.

Leaving the "The Hanging," I realized I had to do something about this. That something was to head on up to a department store for jeans, dungarees, and whatever— not having the slightest notion which was which.

By what circuitous route did I find myself in this age-defying situation at this late stage in my life—eighty-six years old, for Heaven's sake!? I need flash back into how my life traversed those decades before I took this step to purchase "my last dungarees"! Or must it, predictably and in reality, be my last?

CHAPTER 2

The Gift of Chums from the Burning Barn

The Wagon

I was about thirteen years old, the post-overall years, standing in front of Mrs. O'Connor's small grocery store on Hale Street in Beverly Cove, relishing a cool chocolate and vanilla Hoodsie. Nothing was really going on. It was a sunny day, people walking along the sidewalk, heads mostly looking down watching their steps. I sat on the gray, unpainted, uncushioned bench in front of the store, savoring my ice cream cup. As I lifted my head, my eyes caught dark, billowing smoke flowing out of a small round window near the top of the ancient wooden State Public Works barn across the street.

"The barn's on fire!, I shrieked, then stuck my head through the door of the store, pointing upward toward the barn, "It's on fire!" My curiosity in charge, and sensing it would take the town fire engines some minutes to show up, I rushed across the street and around to the other side of the huge barn to see more, but the fire seemed to be mostly still inside. Peeking through a crack in the partly-opened sliding back door— a symbol, I deduced, of the neglect and indifference of the powers-that-be as well as area citizens to this old edifice—I made out the shadows of a chassis of what was once a wagon, remarkably well preserved. It was about fifteen feet long, the bright red-spoked wheels in back twice the size of the front ones. Only the wheels, the iron struts that held the wheels and the front and back together, and the movable shafts for the horse were there. This was a skeleton of the original wagon, missing its body. Why the back barn door was not shut and locked I could only guess: the dilapidated structure and its contents had long ago lost their technological relevance to the then contemporary needs of the Public Works Department. The fire and smoke still must have been contained, perhaps by walls, above the upper floor. I could only suppose that the flames would soon engulf the old, dry wood and quickly destroy whatever was inside the barn.

The moment of decision sent tingles up my spine. Pushing open the door wider, I ran into the barn, and like a horse backing into the gear, picked up two sides of the shafts, one in each hand, and pulled the wagon skeleton out through the door. Taking the back dirt road from the barn, I ran toward Lothrop street about one hundred yards away, the light chassis in tow, the metal bottoms of the wheels bouncing over stones and pot holes. While I may have thought this was not a bad thing to be doing— just saving a junked old wagon from burning— my speed in retreating from the scene revealed my uncertainty on that point. I looked back only when making the turn to the right on Lothrop to see that the barn was being engulfed, but did not return to see the gutted barn until the next day. I spent the early morning gazing at this beautiful, neglected set of wheels, discovering its neatly removable shafts and all. What a find for a nosy, impulsive thirteen year old!

I returned to the scene the next day, to see that the barn was in ruins. I sought commentary on the contents of the barn, or their whereabouts, and heard none. There was too much activity involved in the cleaning up. I found the relief I prayed for. No one cared about the contents. Nobody said word one about a missing four-wheeled, body-less, cast-off chassis.

Eventually, apparently safe to pursue my dream, I thought about what the chums in my youthful gang would think about this skeleton of a vehicle. I wanted to surprise them with it. I found a wide board that would rest on the center of that frame, so that having unclipped the shafts I could sit in front and steer the movable wheels with one foot placed on each side of the axle. This skeleton frame became the instrument of my junk business, my annual chestnut- collecting ritual along Corning Street, and best of all, the endless hours of pleasure and peril for me and my buddies. They would become the engine that made it go. I would "hire" them to sit on the center board by the back wheels and pull on the spokes of the two large back wheels, as I sat in front, guiding the two smaller front wheels with my feet on the axle.

My junk business consisted of collecting newspapers, magazines, discarded copper, brass or other metal piping and such from the immediate residential community, and bringing the load to the garage of my home. Most neighbors were glad to get their collections out of their basements; some preferred to keep the stuff and collect from junk men themselves. After several trips, we would have collected enough to make the call by looking up phone numbers of several listed dealers in town. A quick check of prices per pound for paper, copper or other materials would determine which man to call. On a specified day, the chosen one would show up in an old truck, holes in the back floor boards, the side supports missing pieces; junk dealing was not a highly profitable business.

"Whatcha got this time, young fella?" They got to know me well.

"The usual bundles of newspapers and magazines and some metals," watching him wide-eyed as he adjusted his clanking hand-held scales with the hook on its chain. He would lift the paper bundles by the rope I'd tied them with, and hold it there until we agreed on the number the scale revealed.

"30 pounds," he would say.

"Looked more like 33 to me."

These were crucial moments in these transactions that could make a difference of 20 to 30% in your take.

He'd weigh it again. "O.k., not 33— 32" We settled on 32. I always gave him his call on the review, because I didn't want to irritate him; he might not do business with me again. But I also knew he would cheat me if he could, profit margins being so thin.

Back in 1935, a ten-to-twelve dollar take from one of these collection runs— say ten bundles of papers and magazines and a few pieces of copper— was good money to us. The dollar I would pay each boy who helped me, plus the vast thrill they got riding this flying machine, always sent my chums home happy.

These were just business runs. For recreation, we rode that contraption all over town on the paved public roads, each passenger taking turns steering or pulling at the wheel spokes for locomotion, heading for the longest and fastest hills. On those hills it really was a flying machine. And some of the hills were dangerous to boot, with blind curves and wagon speeds on the smooth pavements that scared and thrilled everyone; hair and loose shirts flying in the wind we stirred up. Oh, I forgot to say: we had no brakes!

On one occasion near the High School football field on Essex Street in Beverly, we got going so fast down the hill that we actually had to pass an old man driving too slow in his car! We had no choice. The alarm on his face as he looked left to see this wild, noisy scene passing him by— *that* had the makings of real heart attack material!

When the season rolled around, my young buddies would gather around for whatever next adventure I had on my agenda. One of them was chestnut collection time. They would gather at our garage on Cross Street and I would load a large 4 by 4 foot plywood box, given to me by a neighbor, onto the center board for a trip along Corning Street to gather up the shiny chestnuts. The entire street was lined with these marvelous trees. I found something really special about the challenge of the prickly cover that invited you to pick up and peel it without sticking your fingers. Plus, the feel of splitting the soft cover, avoiding the prickles, the chestnut skin opening up to yield the glistening, dark brown nut with the light brown circle in its center. Once my friends caught on to avoiding the prickles, which could hurt if you weren't deft about it, they enjoyed the routine and the reward of the just-hatched purity of that bright chestnut.

Once into the fun of it, they were chestnut season regulars for those few young years before we grew into our various more serious sport games.

The added thrill for me and the gang who came with me was the abundance of the supply. Corning Street's twenty-five or so chestnut trees were healthy and prolific, spilling these prickly shells, sometimes with partial stems, by the hundreds onto the street and sidewalks.

I always felt that other young people could appreciate this love affair with chestnuts, especially during the depression years of the thirties when finding anything that remotely resembled a free good was like finding gold.

While I was writing my own memory of this youthful experience, I was surprised and really charmed to find a soul-mate in Westport, Massachusetts, who wrote the following:

"This has been a banner year for horse chestnuts in Westport. The trees flourished and only a few lower branches succumbed to rust, their usual plague. They are loaded with the prickly green capsules containing one or two of the polished nuts. The gale winds the other day blew off so many of the capsules that the lawns and sidewalks under the trees were strewn with some of the biggest, shiniest horse chestnuts I ever saw. I filled my pockets with the best round ones, just as I had when I was a child. In those pre-television years, all proper children guarded their own horse chestnut crop... At this season I carry a horse chestnut in my pocket for luck and give others to people who understand the significance of shiny brown gems. I was shocked to realize that youngsters paid no attention to the wealth on the ground this year.

"I believe one reason I still pick up horse chestnuts is because they are symbols of my happy childhood.... Memory is all we have of our past lives and even though I'm a grandmother...and the horse chestnut tree all but gone, I remember it all when I put the chestnut in my pocket each year. As always, the beautiful luster of a new chestnut doesn't last, but I found an antique knife box of polished cherry wood, shining like a new horse chestnut, and keep my best small knives in it."

Dawn Blake Souza, author of *In Search of Chestnuts*, is a grandmother who knows precisely the content and quality of my own memory about those glistening horse chestnuts on Corning Street.

I would take my huge box of chestnuts, filled to the brim and heavy on the centerboard of that wagon, back to my family garage, where with lots of grunts by my helpers, it was dropped to the garage floor, moved to a safe corner, the contents drawn on by each whenever desired.

Truth be told, we seldom found a true market for those gorgeous, shiny nuts! This was not the roasted edible kind. So, some were passed around to my helpers; others used in fireplaces to bake and crackle and pop when the heat tolerance level was reached, others were passed on as gifts, perhaps placed in some artistic glass container. Many chestnuts were just for feeling and throwing when no one was around. I would say, most of them just rotted away in that box until they were dumped next year when the new season rolled around.

We know that the chestnut tree has been fiercely attacked by a rust disease and has disappeared from many cities, towns and village streets. Nearly all of the trees died on Corning Street years ago. The answer to survival lies in better research and remedy for the plagues that have ravaged the chestnut tree. What kid wouldn't love such a fun tree and its seeds!

The wagon rescued from a burning barn played its part in building that nostalgic memory of when I was just entering my teen years. It became a legend, and after we outgrew this pastime and opted for sports and other pursuits, that wagon remained off in the corner of my backyard in Beverly for a decade or more— the rotting spokes of its wheels beginning to separate, leaving the rusted outer metal rim to hold the skeleton chassis upright.

  The subject of this wagon" and its careening thrills crops up to this day in conversations generated by my old chums, who recall its exploits at reunions in my hometown.

CHAPTER 3
The Cove Gang

The younger chums of the wagon years became part of the pre-jean/dungaree teenage gang I grew up with in the later 1930's. They were sort of immortalized as a community by Jeremiah Murphy, a columnist for the *Beverly Times* when in 1986 he penned the article "Looking Back on the Old Cove Crowd". He called us "a rowdy and delightful collection," and I guess we were. It covered the period of the late thirties when folks were poking into places they'd be embarrassed to find themselves in better times, just to get a crack at even a menial job and wage. Yet our gang, in the prime of expectant youth, found happiness and frolics on the playgrounds and rocky ball diamonds of the struggling towns we played in. We all had part- time jobs cutting someone's lawn, digging artesian wells for the city, or painting houses that had been peeling for years. My job was cutting grass by hand lawnmower; it firmed up my arm and shoulder muscles, which was just what I needed to be a good baseball pitcher.

Just about every family had been hit hard by the Depression, but there were some who had hung on to their jobs at the gigantic United Shoe Machinery plant, the largest source of employment in the whole region— like a giant magnet pulling in available help from surrounding cities. This company work force was doing quite well because they kept their wages at least level while prices had plummeted. Yet, there were no pecuniary distinctions made among our motley crew of off-spring from the area's households; we all somehow looked middle class or lower in our make-shift combinations of homespun tops (we had some time ago graduated from overalls with straps over the shoulders). The well-traveled pants reflected how much we were able to spend on essentials let alone on frivolous items, whether it is clothing or anything else. In that trying era, pot-luck stews became common fare out of the kitchens of the poor.

The members of this Cove Gang did not seem troubled by the times; we were happy playing baseball, basketball and touch football together in leagues sponsored by the New Deal Works Progress Administration Projects. This was the infamous WPA of the less-than-charitable Republican memory of Roosevelt's litany of New Deal welfare jobs. Say what you want about it politically, all I know is that when you ask survivors of that era, they will remind you of what took place in the lives of the many unemployed who eagerly accepted those WPA jobs: the thousands of post offices, bridges, parks, other public facilities that came into being, the paving of hundreds of thousands of roads, the building of fancy walls around public cemeteries, the creating of hundreds of airports—all this between 1935 and 1939 to put people to work and money in their pockets. How history repeats even its worst calamities but decades apart. Few remember that the WPA also noted the sorry plight of writers, artists and actors who struggled in the prevailing malaise of the period, and they put them to work too, writing state and regional guidebooks, gussying up Post Office buildings with colorful and instructive murals, parks with sculptures and theaters with new wave creations. The National Youth Administration emerged to promote sports- sponsored leagues and competitive playoffs to rescue the otherwise idle teen world from wayward pursuits. Playground directors and coaches received some modest fees to cover expenses for their efforts and for trucking us around to nearby (and some not so nearby) towns in their vehicles to meet the game schedules planned in advance. We had games in nearby Peabody, Danvers, Beverly Farms, and even eight or ten miles distant in Salem or Gloucester. I remember a game we played on a rocky/dirt baseball diamond in Hooksett, New Hampshire, which I take from the Atlas map to be about eighty miles from Beverly. We were piled into the back of Coach Ralph Elliott's plumbing truck for the trip up and back. I don't see that game in my scrapbook, so either I pitched and we lost and I ignored the clipping, or we got skunked so bad that no one submitted the game details to our local papers!

But getting back to the *dramatis personae* that Jeremiah was referring to, let me try to capture the characteristics of a few of them just to put further meaning into his description of the group. Putting names to the flesh, minds, souls and behaviors of these cavaliers will help to recall them better too, later. First, let me list them all by alphabet; it's easier to keep track of them. They were: Eddie Adams, "Chink" Brown, Jack and Tom Connor (twins), Billy Collins, Joe Doucette, Edgar Eldridge, Bob Foss, Harry "Fat" Foster, Artie Godfrey, Charlie Gordon, Jimmy Herndon, Cole Hussey, Georgie Janotta, Rut Johnson, Dizzy (Bob) May, Phil O'Reilly, Jimmy Reid, Jack Shea, Mert Ward and myself, i.e. Wardie, Richie— even Eck. I never knew why this moniker.

It is amazing to me that almost seventy years later all of the names and much of the disparate personality traits of that precious crowd still come to mind, along with my vision of their looks. It's as though they never left my memory. Eddie Adams was our smooth basketball player; he made moves as though born to that game, bent toward his goal, sliding through charging bodies with firm control of the bouncing ball, on into the hoop. Though the Cove *Eagles'* best on the court, he seemed from my clippings to have occasionally played with other teams in this sport. Loyalty to a particular team was less essential in those days than getting to play more often. If your team played only one or even two nights a week, that was not enough for some guys and they would hook up with another non-competing league just to improve their game, or even just to get out of the house more nights.

"Chink" Brown was a very special character in this motley Cove Gang. He had been crippled with polio or a similar affliction in his childhood, such that when he walked or ran, his legs and arms sort of flew all over the place, like one might see of a puppet or rag doll being bounced around on a stage. He would show up to play on Ward Four playground in Beverly Cove, and how wonderful it is to relate from memory that in the choosing up of sides to initiate a game, selected Captains and all others would treat Chink no different than anyone else. "I'll take Chink," a Captain taking his turn at picking would say, matter of factly. And, believe me, Chink would be selected by one or another of the teams and he would truly hold his own. This would happen in any of the sports where a bunch of these guys showed up to play baseball or touch football. Though he struggled to control his afflicted muscle system, Chink Brown would be there with his baseball glove or, in touch football, with his big hands ready to throw or snatch a pass. Despite flailing arms and legs, he would get the ground or fly baseball and deal with it, eighty percent of the time. And he would get the bat around—strong arms and wobbly legs cooperating —to send that ball zinging through the infield. In football, even regular tackles, beware, because when he was given the ball to run, that was a sight to watch. It seemed to help him move if he laughed as he ran. With at least one rather boney, flailing arm and both boney legs out there clearing the way, you'd better be careful how you moved in on Chink to stop him or bring him down; get too close to him you'd know you got knocked around on several parts of your body.

The real point in all this is that despite his significant handicap, I firmly believe that there was never a thought in anyone's mind in that wonderful Cove Gang that Chink Brown should be denied the opportunity to play on a par with everybody else.

Jack and Tom Connor were a classy pair of twins that looked so much alike that half the gang called each of them Tom/Jack. Having been a twin who lost his twin sister Betsy at age nine from diphtheria, I was closer to them because his parents gave me special attention and compassion whenever I visited them, often insisting I stay and have dinner with them. Mrs. Connor took great and justified pride in the incomparable soft, puffy white raisin bread she baked and always served hot. Because of this extra time I spent with them, I could distinguish them by a small scar on Tom's cheek and the slight differences in their smiles. Jack was the catcher for our *Eagles* baseball team, and a good one, although his older brother Arthur would occasionally be found behind the plate. All three were good players. Jack is alive as I write. Tom died of cancer years ago, Arthur joining Tom later from a cause unknown to me.

Joe Doucette was a rather special character in this gang. Short, dark curly hair, always ready to grin, a laugh at the ready that consumed him in response to someone's humor. He had a very serious side, deeply religious, always concerned about the family troubles that he would reveal when pressed to explain his occasional gloom. On the other hand, he was so easy to make laugh that he induced antics from me or anyone else near him to play the fool and watch him convulse. He would rather die than hurt someone's feelings. For a five-foot-two guy, he was a good baseball player and did play for other teams on occasion. At the end of my turn, he was elected President of our Cover Athletic Association. For reasons known best to him only, he did not participate in either our basketball or aerial (touch football) contests— just not his thing, being so short and all.

Edgar Eldridge was one of our pitchers and a good one; he won his share of games. As true of everyone else in the sports phase of the lives of members of this gang, almost everyone, including Eldridge the pitcher, was assigned different positions in the field against different teams. Edgar was also considered the brain in the crowd; a good student, serious about his future and, for all we knew, aiming high in whatever career path was on his mind. I have a vague recollection that Edgar had a steady girlfriend back then; he was tall and so was she, and I'm not sure but there is the probability that they married.

Bob Foss was a fair baseball player but not a natural athlete. He had a wry sense of humor, or what came off as humorous when he didn't mean to be funny. This takes talent of the kind that made Jack Benny famous. I remember the Connor twins often saw humor in things Bob would say or do, when others didn't get it. He was truly a nice guy and added a quiet figure to our otherwise often raucous group. Bob is somewhat of an enigma in my memory of his personality and activity. I recall he had a serious crush on a certain dusky-complexioned high school girl and may even have married her later.

Now Harry Foster was someone else again. He picked up the nickname "Fat," because he did carry some excess baggage around the waist. He liked beer, which may have been the culprit, but he was also easy-going and made little attempt to burn off excess anything. Had a good sense of humor and could laugh quietly or hard when called for in response to his own or someone else's observation. He played a decent game of baseball, better in basketball and our aerial touch football games. As one of my best friends in my teen years, we often chummed around beyond baseball, as he lived nearby. Harry's father owned hundreds of acres of farm land near our home on Cross Street where he grew strawberry beds, other vegetables and lots of corn, which in season he cooked for hordes of people there at a well-accoutered cookout station in the field. A lovable man with a responsible position in business, but when on his farm, he loved his ale and the company.

We played a lot of other games besides conventional sports, like kick the can, where whoever is "it"— that is the cop— counts to 50 to give everyone else (the robbers) time to hide somewhere in the woods— in holes, behind rocks or trees. When a robber is found, he flies back through the brush, dead wood, gopher holes and thorny vines to beat the cop to home base, hoping to kick the can before he's tagged by the cop, or "it." Losing, he becomes the next "it". Winning, he yells "allee- allee –in- free," meaning all ye in jail or home base can run free back to the woods. Confusing, but we seemed to know exactly what it all meant then. We played another game of Indian tribes with wooden guns instead of bows and arrows, as being less prone to accidents. The woods for these games were convenient to my house on Cross Street and were indulged in with mixed moods of great intensity and dead seriousness. The game would go on until the team in the woods had all been captured.

Cole Hussey is hard to describe—a true character in his own right. Smirkingly on the border of joke- cracking at all times, you wondered if and when he could be serious about anything. He was lovable because you knew he wasn't sophisticated enough to deliberately hurt anybody's feelings. His clothes always seemed to hang loose about his frame, whether by choice no one would bother to ask; they would just say, "Here comes Cole," and let it go at that. His father owned Hussey's Garage up on Hale Street, a well-respected place to get gas and, more vitally for the neighborhood, to get your car fixed in the mechanical shop in the copious back part of the garage complex. There was nothing frivolous or humorous about Mr. Hussey; he worked hard all day in that garage, mostly in the back, where some serious maintenance jobs were taken care of, like the town's police cars or fire trucks, or a construction company's big trucks or equipment. The huge Department of Public Works barn was right next to Hussey's Garage, and that might have brought some of that business in too, at least until that barn was retired and became a storage place for old DPW equipment, wagons and such. It was five years earlier that it had burned down and the wagon delivered from Hell by yours truly.

Mr. Hussey saw that Cole had a car, which made him especially notable in the Cove Gang, where cars for teenagers were very scarce indeed— maybe two, possibly three old ones in the whole lot of us. This made Cole important, because when members of the gang on a weekend looked to get to a place of fun, like the Gloucester beer house on the wharf twenty -five miles away, the two or three with cars plus, say another, who got permission to take the family wheels, became very popular individuals and were that way most of the prior and following weeks.

George Janotta was unique. Long, lanky, a bit of swagger in his gait. I remember his long fingers when we played agates, earlier called marbles. Smaller agates were put in a ring on the ground and the player with whose turn it was held a much larger agate between thumb and forefinger, so you could snap the thumb off the forefinger trigger-like sending the large agate toward smaller agates in the ring to knock them beyond the ring's edge. Those agates would then be yours. When George Janotta played this game, his grip on the large agate was very different from most other players because he had long, boney fingers that enabled him to cock the large agate in his fingers

21

rather than against his thumb, giving the attacking agate almost bullet speed, enough to knock several small glassy agates out of the ring. Seldom did George lose out in the agate game, and I can see in my mind to this day his long arm, the elbow resting on the ground —the rest of us with smaller fingers simply rested the small finger end of the hand on the ground— his shooting hand twisted and well above ground to get the firing fingers with agate cocked and aimed toward the target in the ring. Kids gathered around the ring to watch George shoot that large agate toward the smaller targets in the ring. He always cleaned up!

He used his long arms and fingers effectively in baseball, too, but did not always show up to play, for some reason. With his frame, he could have been great on our basketball and touch football teams, but these were not sports to his liking. He was part of the gang at other games and events, a bit distant in his ways with the rest of us, but a nice fellow just the same. Though his father was well respected and liked, there was something not quite right in the family. Only years later did I learn that there was a suicide; it wasn't George.

Rut Johnson was our slugger on the Cove A.C. baseball team. He hit home runs just about every game. Short, stocky with red hair and light brown freckles, he was a serious player, not given to horse play or much garrulous banter with other gang members. We all respected his hitting ability and counted on it, but he avoided the frivolous and whacky fun stuff we often indulged in with each other.

Bob "Dizzy" May, it seemed to me, was always grinning about something. A nice fellow, but with a funny or silly bone that gave him his nickname. What he was silly about, I don't recollect, but it was all harmless enough, and easy to take. He blended in with us, usually in our touch football competitions. He rarely played on our baseball or basketball teams, but was successful in his later life.

Phil O'Reilly was one of our best baseball pitchers; had good speed and curve balls, as we called them in those ancient times. He had lost his mother at a young age and lived with his father up on Hale Street. This domestic condition imposed a serious demeanor about life in general, but still he carried underneath all that a good sense of humor, the quirky smile backing it up. Years later he, wife and children visited us in Potomac, Maryland in his Winnebago, all the way from Wisconsin where he had been a salesman. He hated that winter driving and moved to Florida.

Billy Mitchell and Bill Collins were Covers, but were not regular members of our sport teams, in Bill's case because he was a bit young for our level of play. Billy Mitchell had this tic, where he was always pulling up his socks or, in baseball, stockings. You would hardly ever get through a conversation with Billy when he didn't suddenly bend over and pull up his socks, whether they were long or short. Not necessarily just while he was playing ball, but anywhere—in school, standing on the street corner talking to you, in your house, wherever; over he goes forward, bends down and with two hands pulls up his socks. Funny thing to remember, but that was Billy. As for Bill Collins, he told Jeremiah Murphy the "The Cove was the greatest. You had the wide open spaces; it was country, and almost everybody knew everybody else real well. Probably too well." He would laugh.

Finally, Tank Woodbury was distinctive in his nickname, because we used it so regularly that most of us forgot his real name. I know it was Frank, but nobody called him that. He was "Tank" because he was tall, round with soft surfaces. That may well be "fat," but the "Tank" suited him better because when he came barreling down on you in a game of tackles or touch football, this was a tank about to bowl you over. And when you tried to tackle him or push him out of the way as interference for another play, it was like pushing a tank of blubber. It took two to move him at all. All of this good-natured game playing had no malice in any of it. He laughed when it seemed right and played hard when it was called for. Well liked was Tank. Some complained about his perspiring too much—but, hey, nobody's perfect in what is naturally a sweaty game.

Notice in all this, I have said nothing about clothing styles. Just not a factor in describing members of this "rowdy and delightful collection," as Jeremiah tagged them. I remember nothing worth noticing about what they wore, should have worn, or attempted to show off wearing. In such a climate, "style" was not even a common word, as it is today. One thing we didn't wear was jeans, as we know them today. On messy jobs after school or on the week ends out in the yard, farm or wherever any work would get your regular shirt and pants dirty, you might still wear "overalls," though these were more commonly seen on real farmers almost anywhere.

Some reflection of what we must have looked like to others, and felt comfortable even thinking of ourselves, is evident in the names we chose for our teams some years: "The Cove Tramps" was our baseball team name in 1937, before we got busy at the end of that summer and through the winter and raised money for fancy new baseball uniforms. We became *The Cove Athletic Club*, of which I was elected President—that's when the team name, *The Eagles,* got formalized.

As for myself in all this, I labored back then under the delusion that I should be captain of these teams; I had no qualms about speaking up on what we should be doing or how we should go about doing it. There was apparently a sense of purpose in my sportsmanship. In fact and in retrospect, however, I have believed for a long time now that I was made captain of both the baseball and aerial (touch football) teams not just because I played hard and won my share of games and, despite a five -foot- seven frame of average weight, even scored well in basketball and touch football; it was because both coaches and players knew that my father and mother, though never divorced, had separated in 1929, and that my twin sister had died from diphtheria in 1930. In their hearts and souls these lovable roughnecks felt real sympathy for me without saying a word about either of these tragedies in my life.

The special feature of this motley gang was its consistent togetherness in more ways than one. We played these three great sports together week after week in summer and fall, on diamonds and gyms and fields around Beverly, Salem, Gloucester, Peabody and occasionally over the line in New Hampshire, but we also played other games together— not always the same collection, but drawn from the same list: cops and robbers, kicking the can in the woods, volleyball at nearby Blackenberry beach, "tackles" at night in a small field lit by a street light. A smaller contingent drawn from the gang even went out after dark to filch luscious ripe purple grapes from Mrs.

Burrage's backyard vines. I sure remember that one. Suddenly the open back door of her house cast a bright beam toward the vines we were feeding from, I leaped up and started running bent over at first, then stood up to run faster when my neck struck her clothes line. My feet went out from under me as I went down on my back. I escaped but had a sore Adam's apple for a month. What made it worse is that I couldn't tell my mother how it got that way, a sin that felt like a heart burn. On another evening we shifted to Mr. Turner's russet pear trees; boy, were they juicy and good. To vary our fruit diet even more in all this, we would sometimes venture into Mr. Foster's strawberry field, lie down on the hay he spread between the rows to keep the weeds down and began to partake. In the dark, it wasn't easy to make sure you got a ripe one, so we took the bitter with the sweet, the bitter ones puckering the lips and stinging the tongue. And there on his belly in the hay with the rest of us would be Mr. Foster's son Harry, stealing and relishing the illicit strawberries from his own father's crop!

Yes, we were bad, but not the kind of bad you see today. We were relatively harmless bad—the kind that when you tell these tales, people laugh. Today's binge drinking play, drug play or gun play —or some of the other foolishness that goes on among some teens lacking self- discipline— damage people and character, and nobody's laughing.

CHAPTER 4
The Gang Spreads Its Wings

Murphy's "rowdy and delightful cavaliers" hides some important features of this gang. Oh yeah, for a bunch of young teenagers they were smart and they had organizational skills. The evidence is in these 1938 clippings of mine from my scrapbook. I had just turned seventeen and the story speaks for itself:

The Cove Athletic Club, a Beverly Cove young men's group, composed of over a dozen youthful Covers, and managed by Ralph Elliott, local plumber, is one of the most energetic and going organizations in this city. The group also shares good fortune. Last February, the Beverly Cove Improvement Society, interested in the activity of the young men of the community, offered the club the use of what was formerly the caretaker's cottage on the Hunt estate…free of charge as a private clubhouse. The Improvement Society also coupled its offer with a $25 gift to give the boys a start.(In today's dollars, that would amount to about $300.) The clubhouse, a two room two story structure, is equipped with steam heating, running water, electric lighting, a pool table and the necessary furniture, including tables and chairs. The Club's good fortune lies in the fact that this clubhouse is available to them at all times both as meeting and recreation rooms. The Club itself has been organized since last summer. Richard Ward of Cross Street is the President. The Club has taken an active part in the social and athletic functions of the Cove sector, sponsoring *several whist parties held at Cove School, and a uniformed baseball team. Plans are already underway for this seasons nine. Five new uniforms have been purchased and the first game will take place on May 7 at Nashua, N.H.*

Tomorrow night, the club will conduct an informal dance at the Cove School, the proceeds of which will go to help finance this year's diamond activity. Music will be provided by the Colony Club orchestra under the Direction of Bill Publicover, popular leader and soloist. A large gathering is expected.

Officers are pictured around the pool table, hands gripping poles, several sporting neckties. As the gang made its way through Beverly High School, each developed separate interests and took up with the girls. We often teamed up on dates and gathered at house parties or cafés where music, dancing and beer sparkled the evening's activity.

It was during the latter part of those high school years, while not neglecting our sport events that I chose to participate in plays and musicals. I find in my scrapbook: "Beverly High School Presents its third Inter-Class Dramatic Competition, December 9, 1938." I played the part of "Maharajah" in *The Command Performance*. Apparently I came by this part when the person originally assigned the part dropped out. The journalist wrote: "There has been one change in the cast of the play: Richard Ward has taken over the part of Maharajah. He has had this part but a short time and is doing a remarkable piece of acting in its presentation." My own recollection of my performance was far less complimentary; to be honest I thought I was terrible. Capturing the tones, the feel and the oily aura of an Oriental potentate was not easy for me—and in my gut I felt it showed.

Now, the musical was different. "Ye Olde Plantation Minstrels" was a major production of over- fifty singers and dancers. I sang in the Beverly Young Men's Republican Club Quartette, courtesy of my brother George's involvement in that party's politics as President of the Club. Blame James Michael Curley, the quintessential Boston Irish politician, who had stamped the word Democrat on the Ward family psyche in those days. While I lean now to the more socially sensitive attitudes of that party toward the vulnerable in our society and the world, I eschew party membership and examine the spectrum of views of each candidate and choose without being fettered to politics or party. I believe my late brother George had, in fact, been the only member of the Ward clan to sign up as a Republican, finding advantage to him at that time and place in doing so. His views wavered later in life.

Anyway, getting involved in these community events influenced dress codes. As I said, Our gang members and families were all struggling through the depression years. Money was scarce, jobs were scarce, but everybody found work, as teenagers today are expected to do. Yard caretaking for two estates in my home town kept me busy; I cut many miles of grass in my teen years, raked leaves, cultivated gardens. These were not riding mowers; I walked, always in my non-descript work clothes. As I said, jeans or dungarees as we know them now were not part of our lives. Absent a father, my eldest brother Ralph, ten years my senior, was as close a surrogate as I could wish; he bought me a brand new, shiny-black balloon tire bicycle. It was the rage then, and I was in heaven. I rode my bike a mile or so to each job and back. Other gang members dug artesian wells or worked at garages, stores or on farms. The physical conditioning of those years was special, because in the course of a week, gang members went from a variety of menial jobs to playing baseball during the day or basketball at night. We also walked a mile or so to our schools daily. No buses for those within a mile of the school. We were all in great shape.

It was a different story when we were engaged in our club's events to raise money for uniforms: the dances, the whist parties, selling tickets, having member pictures taken for the newspaper. For these occasions we dressed up. We wore ties and jackets, as we did when dating. Rehearsals for plays and musicals weren't casual.

A major transformation took place in my life soon after my graduation from high school. My older siblings were already in college. My brother Ralph was at Boston College on Scholarship for his speed on the track, Sister Lucy at Simmons College, working in her spare time as a governess for the Saltonstall family in Topsfield. Brother John, also at Boston College, covered his room and board as a caretaker at the Philomethia Club. Brother George at Northeastern Law nights, worked days for Trowt's Packard Dealership in Beverly Farms. It was determined that I was lacking two vital courses to qualify for the better colleges. Lucy had it in her head that I should go to Harvard. I could only smile and feel puffed up at her loving confidence in me. I lacked Trigonometry and Physics. The financial burden on the family, due to parental separation, was horrendous. My father had in the prosperous '20's built us a beautiful, classic American home on an acre-and-a-half of land, with an orchard behind of russet pear, apple, cherry and peach trees, leafy arbor ways of white and purple grapes, spacious garden space for flowers and vegetables, a long well- built shed for pets or farm animals we chose to tend— all of it shadowed by a row, along the back of the lot, of sixty-foot-plus pointed spruce trees. Nice, but without adequate alimony to support the estate, there was much neglect in maintenance. Yet, instead, my hard-working Irish mother, though left alone to cope with seven children under seventeen, beamed at the sight of all of us either in or headed for college, a privilege that neither she nor her husband could indulge. The beauty of the place was a joy, but the financial struggle to educate her brood was a constant on her mind too. In these circumstances, it would help the family marginally if I delayed college for a year. Besides, it gave me the shot at taking those two courses I needed and the time to earn some cash savings.

I returned to Beverly High for Trigonometry in the Fall term, 1939, and found a Boston College Professor of Physics we knew nearby to take me on. I would maintain my jobs and ponder the options about which college to attend as the year went on. My brother had started his own floral business and I spent much time working for him, delivering products and tending his retail outlets. By January, 1940, with a good grade in the Trig course, I had only Physics to bone up on. Spring was busy time for my brother's business as well, so my schedule was full. Summer and fall of 1939 and spring, 1940 became a working, studying, reading period. I fell in love with the great classic novels and biographies and became enamored of writing styles. I wanted to be a writer! I played the sedulous ape to many an author, whose style I thought worth imitating. It would be a while before I could really get to writing for publication.

As summer approached, my brother George asked me if I would be interested in taking a job as a Page in the Massachusetts Legislature. As President of the Beverly Republican Club, he knew a local banker who was in strong with a number of state legislators. I could hardly wait. When the Legislature met in the fall of 1940, I would be a page in the House of Representatives in that famous State House with the golden dome in Boston. I was eighteen years old. It really did transform my life. It lifted me out of my parochial world into a year of fascinating exposure to the politics of state government in one of the oldest political institutions in the country. I commuted from Beverly Cove's Montserrat station. Another page lived in Gloucester, several stations before mine, and we became close friends on that commute. We would walk from North Station up the hill to the State House, arriving at work at 8:00 am. Sargeant-at-Arms employees wore dark uniforms with brass buttons, so there would be no confusion about our rights of passage as we moved about the legislative chambers or offices of the State House delivering messages, or fetching information for legislators.

One of my jobs was to keep the Speaker's office legislative bills in order. I used the opportunity early in the morning before staff appeared to learn to type, using Gregg's typing manual. I have been a rapid-fire typist ever since. Christian Herter was the speaker of the House, a wonderful gentleman— stately, a magnificent voice, commanding respect from all irrespective of party affiliation. Pages keep all legislative bills up-to-date at the desk of each representative. Each morning, five or six legislative pages with fitted rubber fingers would walk along the side of a long table piled with copies of all the legislative bills likely to come before the house. The Senate had its own page staff and would be doing the same. I was enthralled with the variety of duties in this job, which included being available to legislators when the House of Representatives were in session.

Everyday was an excitement, especially when debates heated up. When governors from various states came to the State House, I collected their autographs: Leverett Saltonstall of Massachusetts, Governor Lehman of New York, Frank Dixon of Alabama, Charles Farrow, Virgin Islands. Some of the signatures are indecipherable.

I sat in on the impeachment trial of Dan Coakley, mesmerized by the tall, black, Lincolnesque barrister who weighed in, though I don't recall whether for the defense or prosecution. I was appalled at how noisy the great House hall could be during some sessions, when a Representative would be talking but nobody listening. I was disgusted by the sight of spittoons by each desk, the cigar smoking and actual frequent use by some members of those ugly receptacles. I was impressed by the eloquence of some members with a cause. It was an incomparable education in state politics.

During the summer, my sister's campaign to get me into Harvard went into full swing. She helped me fill out the voluminous paperwork, craft the essays required, obtain letters of recommendation. She helped me prepare for the College Board examinations held at Beverly High School. Arriving early afternoon for the test on American History, I was told that that test was given in the morning. The afternoon test was on European History, my favorite subject. I was permitted to take it. I followed up with a trip to Cambridge to talk to the Dean of Students about my *faux pas* in timing on the American History test. My diligence in following up on that must have impressed somebody. By mid-fall I had everything completed, still doubting a positive response. My grades were good, but not outstanding. My outside activities and leadership roles in both sports and in the community among my peers was fairly impressive. My trip to Cambridge demonstrated strong desire.

As I had become somewhat acquainted with Christian Herter in and around his office and yet just a page, I believe I had established a reputation for diligent work on the job. Though I never saw the letter, I was told he sent one. A prominent Harvard man himself from a most distinguished family long connected with Harvard, that letter may well have done the trick; I will never know. All I know is, by the spring of 1941 I had been admitted to Harvard College, to commence in the fall. My sister's incredible belief in me paid off— one of only three from Beverly High School that year to have that honor of getting into Harvard. Later, Speaker Herter became Governor of Massachusetts and subsequently U.S. Secretary of State.

Getting into Harvard is one thing, staying in is another. I commuted from Beverly my first year. Every morning I walked 20 minutes to Montserrat Train Station, took the 7:20 to North Station, the subway to Cambridge, checked in to my locker in Dudley Hall— the Commuter's facility on campus— hustled off to my 9 am class. It was a grind, but it was free of the distractions of residence living. I spent much of my weekends studying, just to stay afloat. When first confronted with the assignments, I thought they were for the month. The amount of reading seemed impossible to complete in one week. Every Monday morning there was a History I test on the previous week's work. Elements of that wonderful course still spill forth from my memory on certain subjects that arise in debate even now. Each course was demanding of full attention, at least given the level of the public high school courses I had experienced.

My experience as a Page in the State House prepared me well for the dress code on the Harvard campus in those days, so very different today. Then jackets and ties were common around the campus and in class. Students from some of the private schools could even be seen sporting straw hats in spring, as they strutted across the yard toward class or the library. There were a variety of slacks, but jeans were certainly not the uniform of the day in those days. As for Dungarees— forget it!

Somehow, I found a way to make it through that arduous first year, determined not to jeopardize what was for me a miracle of good fortune to have the opportunity. The family's resources and borrowing capacity were strained to the limit to come up with my tuition payments and then my residence expenses when, in the second year, I moved into Winthrop House. I did not share the fancy dining privileges (jackets and ties on special occasions), as I could not afford them. At different times I worked for my meals in Harvard's freshman dining hall kitchen and waited tables in Cambridge restaurants.

One good thing: campus life did open the door for me to get involved in college activities. One of those activities was baseball. All of that experience with my home town team seemed to portend well for a chance to play for Harvard. In the spring of my sophomore year, I prepared a brief with clippings of my many successful pitching games, including the one showing that I had made the cut on the Beverly High School team. That sort of validated your status as at least a pretty good player. When I got the notice to show up at Brigg's Cage for a try out at Soldier's Field, Harvard's athletic complex in Cambridge, I was floating on a cloud.

CHAPTER 5

The Call to the Mound at Fenway— and from Uncle Sam

At Brigg's Cage, heavy netting was hung from the ceiling and strewn about to allow batters to take full swings at the baseball. The nets were also strung up to protect other players from batted balls, as pitchers and catchers, infielders and outfielders warmed up in other parts of the Cage. Baseballs were flying all over the place in a space about as big as half a football field, but everyone felt safe with the netting arrangement.

Baseball coach Floyd Stahl was about 5' 4", but no matter, he was in charge. I knew it was a challenge for me to make this team, but I intended to give it all I had. When I wasn't pitching myself to an assigned catcher, I was moving about— as a catcher for other pitchers warming up, or just playing catch to warm up outfielder arms and my own. I took my turn in the batting cage, feeling a little short myself at 5' 7" against Harvard pitchers of six foot and more, so if the coach was to be impressed with me, it had to be the pitching or, possibly, outfield positions. As a pitcher, I had excellent control, seldom walking batters, a good but not overpowering curve ball, a good change-up and a fair sinker. I was early on labeled a "utility pitcher" without being too sure exactly what that meant. Just being useful, I guess, without firm commitments as to my status. Would I make it? Hang around, lots of hustle —and let's see.

We were scheduled to play the Red Sox in Fenway Park in nearby Boston in an exhibition game on April 16 that spring of 1943. This produced a high level of excitement and anticipation. For Stahl, it was undoubtedly a worrisome effort to get everyone ready; he would want the team to make a decent showing against Joe Cronin's potent Red Sox. The likes of Bobby Doerr, Eddie Lake, Skeeter Newsome, Big Jim Tabor, Tony Lupien, Tex Hughson, Joe Phelan, Johnny Peacock, Roy Partee, and aging Al Simmons posed a daunting opposition. Yet Stahl thought his rigorous practices in the Cage the week prior to the game would prepare his team well for combat on the big day.

The whole story of this event was written up in the *Harvard Bulletin* of April 27, 1968: "When Harvard Played the Red Sox." Until I received this Harvard Alumni *Bulletin* article, my info was that Harvard played the Red Sox in exhibition in early spring *every year*, which, if it had been true, would render my tale fairly common knowledge. But it wasn't. In fact, as of 1943 the only other time Harvard played the Red Sox in pre-season exhibition was in 1916, when Harvard's Ned Mahan beat the Red Sox on five hits, 1-0!

Anyway, I was so awed by the Fenway atmosphere that I could hardly concentrate on the task the coach called out to me to do.

"Take the fungo bat, "he shouted across the diamond to me, "belt some fly balls out to the Harvard outfielders!" A fungo bat is specially made long and thin to allow for hitting the ball high and long. You had to have a "good eye" to hit them right because the bat is really thin, almost like a stick. But I had done quite a bit of this growing up, hitting rocks with a stick and baseballs with a fungo bat in our hometown league. The precision called for in putting that long, thin, round, smooth piece of wood on the baseball you threw up in the air in advance of your swing was a joyous challenge. Stahl recognized I was adept at this and gave me the task. Naturally, he would sympathize with my relatively short stature and try to keep me busy, catching pitchers, batting to fielders and doing a little warming up as a pitcher myself.

One of the Harvard pitchers I enjoyed catching in warm-ups was Bud Mains who had a killer fast ball; your catching glove hand had to be tough to take it. And in early spring, your glove hand's palm was not tough, so it would swell for weeks before hardening up. Later in the game with the Red Sox, Mains would strike out Lake, Doerr and Cronin. Bud could also be wild, so on the second round of hitting in the game Cronin chose not to go up against him, thinking getting hit by that ripping fast ball from an amateur—not good.

Soon, the Red Sox batters were taking their warm-ups and it was their star pitcher Tex Hughson loosening up on the mound. Tex went to the minor leagues from college, but he soon made it to the big leagues and eventually in 1941 to the Red Sox. That year his record was 5 wins, 3 losses, not all that impressive. But he blossomed with a record of 22 and 6 in 1942, 18-5 in '43 (the year we were playing the Sox) and 20- 11 in 1946, when they won the Pennant! His prize statistic: he never lost a 1-0 game in the major leagues, winning all seven of those games with the Red Sox, according to my source (a *Boston Globe* article in my scrap book of March 14, 1984). It was "the best record of this kind in Red Sox history." He came down with a sore arm in 1947, claiming too much spotty bull pen work, and hung up his glove and ball for good in 1950. As the story goes, he loved pitching in Fenway Park so much that in his subsequent Texas Real Estate enterprise he named Boston streets in his developments: "Fenway Park," "Beacon Street," "Commonwealth Avenue," and so on.

I dwell on Tex here because as he finished his warm-ups on the mound and started walking off, Coach Stahl— out of the blue— directed me to the mound to warm up the Harvard batters. He knew my control was notable and felt I wouldn't waste a lot of pitches trying to get the ball over the plate. The idea was to give the batters something good to hit! And I did. Right down the middle mostly.

My mates pounded the ball all over the place and I knew they felt good. Even if I could have beefed up my delivery in order to impress somebody, that's not what the coach wanted and certainly not what our batters wanted. So I fed them straight fast balls but down the middle, and they happily creamed my pitches.

Stahl was a gentleman and a humanitarian. He appreciated and liked my diligent play but knew full well I would not have the stuff to make the team. Using me in many roles was a fatherly gesture that I never forgot, and I regret not getting back to him then or years later to tell him how l felt about pitching in Fenway Park. The other regret that lingers in my aging mind is that had I known I might join the team in Fenway Park and even get to pitch from the mound, I would have roped a family member to show up with a camera! There are, as Frost says, roads not taken; there are also pictures not taken. This was a precious picture not taken, and though the story is there, the Fenway pictures were lost to my scrap-book!

The final results of that game? Red Sox 21, Harvard 0. My warm-ups for the Harvard batters made them look good but certainly didn't prepare them well for the big league pitching of Ken Chase, Andy Karl and Norm Brown, each of whom shut the Harvard batters down. Personally I thought we weren't swinging enough. But then, we seemed befuddled when we did swing. The only glory for Harvard was that feat of Bud Main's striking out the side and later signing with the Philadelphia Athletics the following summer. Harvard's pitcher, Warren Berg, and his catcher, Ed Fitzgibbons, were signed to minor league contracts to the Red Sox's Scranton Farm Team.

All good times come to an end. That experience will always live in memory and is passed on both in my scrap book clippings and this narration. At the end of the sophomore year, a real transformation took place in my life— a literal sea change. It was occasioned earlier by the bombing of Pearl Harbor by the Japanese on December 7, 1941. The U.S. Government had launched military programs on college campuses around the country. One of them was the Navy V-12 officer's training program. On July 3, 1943, we were first inducted in Eliot house yard into the U.S. Naval Reserves as Seamen 1st class, handed our uniforms and other gear, and moved into the Eliot House dorm. There was something jaunty about the seaman's garb—a dark shade of blue, with the large collar hanging down the back with the white thin stripes that flapped in the wind. The bell bottom trousers really made you want to show off. The uniform, it was widely touted, really aroused womenfolk. If I'm not mistaken, and I probably am, I think I was too busy struggling to take in all the subtle peripherals—and pass all the courses too!

Just prior to our induction, Eliot House had been one of the most expensive and elitist housing units on campus. Our regular class schedules continued, except for adding a couple of courses deemed relevant for future naval service: Navigation, Astronomy, Mechanical Drawing, Physics—all good, interesting stuff. The biggest change in our lives? We were regimented 24-7. You could no longer leave the campus and go wherever you wished, whenever you wished. You were in the U.S. Navy for the rest of the war. You were Uncle Sam's boys!

The most startling miracle for the family after July, 1943 was that the government picked up the tab for everything! Tuition paid, housing paid, food paid, clothing paid, books paid. Gifts from God and Uncle Sam! The other bonus was that I no longer needed to work for my meals and other daily living expenses. This arrangement carried through for the remainder of my Harvard education. In the spring of 1944, as advanced seniors, we were shipped off to Asbury Park, New Jersey for an interim stay, until Columbia University's next Midshipman School class session was available for our contingent from Harvard. For all of us, it was the beginning of yet another chapter: we were being prepared as officers targeted for real active duty in the Pacific Theater of War.

For the three years I served in the Navy, nary a single piece of clothing did I have to worry about buying. At the same time, I had no choice in what I might prefer to wear— nothing resembling jeans or dungarees. You wore "regulation G.I." for your role in the Navy— for the duration. Once officers, the seaman's outfit was history. Both the dress-up Navy Blues with gold braid on the cap with visor and the everyday grays were classy outfits. In summer, there was the optional white-topped cap's visor. You couldn't help but feel good about yourself. The only dress-downs we were allowed to knock around in off duty recreation were cotton sweat suits.

My active war years after leaving Harvard in '43 are pretty thoroughly covered in my *Grampas Are For All Seasons* book and compares, though perhaps less heroically, with experiences of many who found themselves in that troubled area. We did engage at Okinawa, claimed by noted historians, one of the largest, most significant, yet unheralded battles in the entire war. Winston Churchill said as much. The onslaught on the beaches was like Hell itself had exploded: battleships pouring out steady, streaking reams of fire power from the massive 16-inch guns, the 40 and 20 millimeters spewing smoke as they cracked away at diving Japanese Kamikaze suicide pilots, their motors screaming as many of their planes crashed with violent fireballs, either into the sea, missing their targets, or into many U.S. ships. As Assistant Gunnery Officer in charge of the 20 mm guns on my own ship, as well as being the Recognition Officer trained to identify foe from friendly plane, I ordered all gun stations to fire at anything that came anywhere near us, the billows of smoke from the expansive imbroglio making such distinctions impossible. All of this, though like a Hollywood staged scene, was more than hot enough for my liking.

Everything after Okinawa seemed anticlimactic. The struggle for the island went on with historic, significant consequence for the military, for the United States, Japan and the world. The Japanese government would not surrender in the conventional manner of the defeated. They would fight to the last citizen of their country, if necessary. Their binding code to their troops and people was to fight to the last man, woman and child, even expecting parents to kill their young offspring rather than turn them over to the hated enemy. They would commit every citizen on mainland Japan to die for their homeland rather than yield. Suicide became for them a national policy of State, in terms of scale unique in human history. The air Kamikaze attacks were but a partial symbol of that policy. The casualties in an event of non-surrender would have been stupendous in numbers—American and Japanese—including also those hundreds of thousands of allied military who were held in concentration camps. Historians writing in retrospect and with revealing documentary evidence have concluded that President Truman's decision to use the atomic bomb to bring Japan and its people to their knees and to final surrender probably saved millions of military and civilian lives on both sides, even as the atomic bombs themselves took their ghastly toll. Shipmates speculated that they, too, would have been among those dead had the invasion of Japan been necessary. The philosophical debate on the efficacy of resorting to use of the atomic bomb will no doubt continue with something less than conclusive surety.

For those of us involved, sailing away from Okinawa brought speculations about what the immediate future would entail, in terms of eventually returning to civilian life and normal pursuits. There was uppermost in mind the fact that we will have survived the worst of the war's violence, provided the atomic bomb had produced the desired decision on the part of the Japanese Generals and the Emperor. After the German surrender in the summer of 1945, and Japan, in a sense, on the ropes, one could start transitioning mentally to one's future. For most, it would entail returning to loving families and places where we felt at home again. Soon after the return welcoming and embedding in civilian routines, new priorities would emerge in the matter of completing one's academic degree or training, while pondering options in a career path and setting exciting and desirable goals. The pragmatics of getting a job, would occupy the mind.

All of that mental planning would have come second to thoughts of eventually getting back home again and being with family and old friends, but those second thoughts would not be trivialized nor neglected.

Chapter 6

The Search for Love and Direction

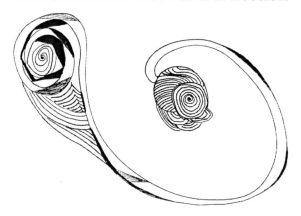

How did the State of Michigan ever get into this picture? Or Ann Arbor and the University of Michigan? Just one of those unexpected, unplanned, unenvisioned moves that happen in life. Following a post-war summer at Harvard finishing up my degree, I had found a job at a Public Relations firm on Boylston Street, moved into an apartment on Beacon Street with a home town friend, then a company CPA, who had been in the Harvard Navy V-12 program. We would scavenge around the back alleys behind the apartment building for empty fruit or produce crates as wood for our fireplace.

All of this background played into my Public Relations job, as I wrote scripts for sponsors advertising on radio and felt satisfied hearing my words fed back to me when my scripts were used. Sometimes the job took bizarre turns. For the June Dairy Month account, I held a milk cow's head harness while the photographer snapped away, feeling lucky I wasn't asked to hold the tail, like in dog shows.

As spring 1947 rolled by, I became restless and was beginning to envision a dead-end career. The fresh breezes of new hope and inspiration struck me that I needed more education; I needed some specialization that gave me a foundation for my opinions. A basic liberal arts education at the bachelor's level, even from Harvard, would hardly raise convictions above that of the dilettante. So, graduate school loomed as the answer.

Ah, but which graduate school? Which specialization? That took some pondering. Logic brought into focus my undergraduate major in college. That was a start in the direction of specializing. If not my preferred field, a major in Economics could be built on, if the subject matter could but capture my interest and enthusiasm. It seemed the most practical thing to do. I loved literature and the idea of a writing career but realized that lacking enough undergraduate coverage in literature, history and writing I'd be wrapped up for two years getting just the Master's degree, whereas my preparation in Economics would produce a Masters in that field in a year. I thought of the Harvard School of Business, too, as a short-cut to success, but thinking about it decided it was too narrow a focus. I applied and was admitted to the University of Michigan, having read that it was deemed by some, at least in that part of the world, as the Harvard of the Midwest. I knew by the recognized names of the professors in Economics that it had an excellent graduate program in that field.

Before making the binding commitment to Economics, and to satisfy my penchant for literature—I thought of it as the dessert of the intellect— I enrolled for the summer school session of 1947 in the famed Breadloaf School of Literature and Writing at Middlebury College in Vermont, using the generosity of the G.I. Bill offered veterans of World War II. The courses in Literature— English Ballad, Chaucer, Poetry, Drama, Writing and Shakespeare—would fill the hunger that helped compensate for the long road I had chosen toward a Ph.D. in Economics. At the end of that summer, I had completed twelve credits or so toward the Master's Degree in English at Breadloaf. It felt good; I wouldn't become just an Economics nerd, but rather at least a quasi- renaissance man.

There was an additional incentive for studying at the University of Michigan in Ann Arbor in the fall. Sister Lucy had married a man from Elkhart, Indiana. She needed, I felt, a family member nearby. I could visit her fairly easily on occasion, hitching rides if necessary from Ann Arbor. I took the train from Boston to Ann Arbor with one suitcase of clothing and other personals, found a rooming house run by a nice Italian lady near the Michigan hospital, shared the room with another graduate student. Here again, the G.I. Bill paid all tuition, books, academic supplies, plus a monthly stipend of $135. I found a job in a woman's dormitory near my room which nicely took care of all meals. I bought a bicycle to get around the campus. The year went by fast. As expected I completed the requirements for the Master's degree in Economics in the year, still not certain where that would take me. I looked forward to being home in Beverly again with family, for the summer at least.

Perhaps I should think about teaching. What institution would take a Master's degree credential as sufficient for college teaching? I went out to Cambridge to browse around in the Harvard Placement Office and bulletin boards to check out the listings.

"Bates College Seeks Instructors in Economics."   Bates is a small college in Lewiston, Maine. I armed myself with letters of recommendation, one from Joseph Schumpeter— one of the world's leading economic theorists whom I had as a Professor at Harvard. I doubt that he remembered me or even was concerned about the B+ grade he gave me, but gentleman and humanitarian that he was he wrote a fine letter of recommendation. Arriving at Bates College by train —I still had no car— I felt confident about the job with that letter in my briefcase, though upon arrival, was somewhat dismayed by my initial impression of the city. To the left and right there were the stained, dank walls of the textile mills, the pungent chemical odors wafting from the Androscoggin River and canals, into which companies spewed waste chemicals derived, I learned later, from production processes. Then, approaching the campus area, its quaint beauty and academic aura, the well-kept homes, grounds and residence halls, the College President's stately home— all revived my spirits. I had a cab take me around other parts of the city and found many other residential areas pleasing enough.

The long interview was accomplished with the Dean of the College, a true Down Mainer, who sprinkled his conversation with many "impawtint" things; the job was mine. The salary was $2500 an academic year; the housing was up to me to find. I prefer to live with a family, when possible, and found a perfect home with a fine upstairs room, just a seven-minute walk from the building where I would be teaching. All arrangements made, I went back to Breadloaf for the summer of 1948, realizing that it would be my last hurrah for literature, per se.

I returned to Bates in the fall to begin my college teaching career. During the course of that year in Lewiston, two important events took place. I met my future spouse, who was a radio personality in town, and decided to commit to becoming a college professor. The freedom of the daily schedule, the independence of being your own specialist and controlling the content of your work, the breaks in the school year and in summer for undertaking alternative pursuits related to your profession, switching out of the heavy winter wear essential for surviving the Maine freezes with "ears so cold they could chip off." There was much to love about the contrast in life modes except, of course, the poor salaries. By the time the first year was up, while not committed to marry, plans were percolating in my head. I spent a summer at Seattle University resolving some War Time associations when living there, then returned to Bates for the second and last year teaching in Lewiston, Maine. My career at Bates ended in June of 1950 and I prepared to return to Ann Arbor to complete the Ph.D. program in Economics. Cecilia and I were engaged in the fall. In Ann Arbor, I would put a year in on the graduate course work, still living in the same rooming house, but now with a graduate student also in Economics. The wedding plans were set for September of 1951.

The year apart while Cecilia worked at WLAM and I hunkered down on my course work was not easy, but with a marriage goal set, we could relax in one another's love and anticipation of our wedding and focus on our respective jobs. After the wedding took place the following September, we honeymooned briefly in Boston and Cape Cod and prepared to travel back to Ann Arbor and found an apartment. Just behind the University's impressive Law School building on Oakland Street we found the ideal place: a basement apartment in a privately owned red-brick home, with large bedroom and living room, kitchenette, bathroom and our own private entry.

It felt homey because a loving family, a tailor and his wife, occupied the upper part of the house. Cecilia was comforted by having an older lady in the same house, for company and for reasons of mutual safety or health.

We settled in fast. Cecilia found a job at the local radio station WNEW, while I pursued my graduate work and looked for another job to supplement our income, made up of Cecilia's radio salary and my G.I. monthly stipend of $135. Close budgeting, but we had enough and we were happy, very happy. Even so, I needed to find an extra income source, and with the help of my former roommate, who had applied to the massive Willow Run factories, outside of Detroit, I got a job there too. This is where the famed WW II B-24 Liberator bomber had been produced, and after the war, the Kaiser-Frazer automobiles.

A little history is called for here, because Willow Run played a very special role as part of the great "Arsenal of Democracy" that was Detroit in that Great War. Catching up on the past of the place made me realize so much more now than I did at the time what a privilege it had been to have worked in that vast hall of memory at Willow Run, the site once said to have been but a sleepy hamlet and creek and summer camp for underprivileged boys. To address the might of German ambitions and its war machine, the United States government commissioned Henry Ford to build the factory, "the largest building in the world at the time" (1942), producing nearly 500 of the huge "Liberator" bombers. Five million women were rapidly brought into the labor force in the country, twelve thousand of them to the Willow Run complex alone. They had been teachers, waitresses, nurses, actresses, copy editors, at home mothers from all walks of life and were trained quickly to become welders, riveters, crane operators, parts distributors, quality inspectors. Instead of skirts on the job they wore trousers— overalls/coveralls, jeans, dungarees still not yet the rage.

When the war ended, Henry Ford no longer needed this plant and leased it to former President of Graham-Paige Motors, Joseph Frazer and industrialist Henry J. Kaiser. They joined talents to build some different automobiles, like the big Kaiser sedan, the conventional size Frazer, the small Henry J, the Darrin Sports car and eventually adding Willys and Jeep lines to their empire. This was the only auto maker to achieve success after World War II, at least for a decade or so. It was for the Kaiser-Frazer auto production operation at Willow Run that my friend and I were hired. The trauma and demands of the war brought a transformation in the work place that was destined to impart permanent features to the factories and work places of the future. For example, women continued to make up a large segment of the factory labor force in a variety of roles they had mastered during war production. They were not necessarily the same women, but the new hires inherited the new workplace atmosphere.

Everyone was required to join the union; the progress made on behalf of organizing unions during the 1930's, buttressed by the Wagner Act of 1935, assured that outcome. My graduate friend and I worked on the late shift, 4 p.m. to midnight. It was clean work, inside, comprised of many hundreds of male and female workers. Lots of sheet-metal parts as well as complicated auto parts were being fashioned and used in their jobs by employees, irrespective of gender. The work force was about 40% female—men and women working side by side at most production sites.

My partner, who had led me to the job opportunity, was assigned to work in the rafters somewhere, pulling out long metal rods and other pieces as ordered by the production units below, while I found myself assigned to a very large automobile parts cage. Here, workers from various production areas would come to replenish the parts they needed to produce the car sections they worked on. As workers came to the Cage's open window to order parts, I would be sent to where the parts were stored and stashed, pull them out and deliver them to the worker at the window. Not rocket science, as they say. The job gave me ample time to sit in back of the stacked parts, either to read a class assignment, or write a paper or a book review. A number of these book reviews appeared in what is now called *The Review of Social Economy*, a publication of the Association for Social Economics. I also completed an article back there in the stacks for the *History of Michigan* Journal.

What was more important to my daily work in that giant factory was my writing for the Union newspaper, distributed weekly within the plant. It was widely read, so I became somewhat of a known quantity around the factory. My articles tried to deal with controversial issues, like the new role of women in factory life. They were out there working side by side with men in just about all phases of the work being done. In one article, I spoke to the issue of how women should and could maintain their feminine role while functioning within a macho male factory floor environment. As many of the women were mothers, I tackled head-on how they should set a standard of behavior that did not breech the patterns one would expect of a mother of children. Just because they were in the same work clothes as the men—coveralls or denim work pants, whatever—they did not have to take on or accept the cursing, sexual banter or crude jokes men were often willing to freely exchange with them. The role for women was to bring a more civil tone and conversation to the factory scene. This was all in one article, which caused quite a stir and generated some exchanges with me at the parts cage counter. The working environment was not easy for women who were sensitive to the harsher social environment they were forced to work in. Every week I came up with topics emanating from the common gossip among the factory work force. I gained some sense of power within the union and among management, not because they worried about my influencing policy or radical changes of rules of behavior between union and management, but simply because they weren't sure what topic I was going to address next, nor whether it would have any effect on the work force or on decisions from the upper echelons of management. It was a heady time for me, being just another factory employee, but becoming known as somewhat of a maverick with troubling—from my viewpoint, progressive—ideas.

This Willow Run factory experience with a broad spectrum of the so-called "working class" was a valuable antidote to the student/academic world that engrossed the other half of my daily life. During my course work, I had been an assistant to Professor William Haber, correcting piles of his blue book exam papers each semester. He was also one of my mentors on my doctorate committee, another true gentleman and humanitarian— one of the most considerate student-oriented professors I ever had.

Once I had completed nearly all of my graduate course requirements for the Ph.D., I was focused on preparing for and passing the Comprehensive exams that cleared the way for selecting, writing and defending the doctoral dissertation. I really enjoyed these two sides of my working and academic life— my feet on the ground half a day at Willow Run, my head in the clouds the other half on the university campus: laborer and student. At the same time my wife also led a double life: working at the Ann Arbor Radio station, WNEW, and also pregnant and preparing herself for motherhood. We met in the mornings before she went to work. As I was home half a day, but at work through the evening hours, it would be one a.m. before she felt the presence— my having returned from the four-to-twelve shift at Willow Run— of her man in bed.

Naturally, the attire I wore to the factory contrasted with my daily student garb. Working pants and tops were replaced with the typical student slacks, shirts, sweaters, pullovers common to the breed.

Despite these hectic schedules Cecilia and I followed, we still managed to entertain friends in our apartment and to socialize with them at other gatherings and events. We lived a full, happy life. This comfortable routine was disturbed in the spring of 1952 when I failed one section of the doctoral comprehensive exams. This was my own doing, as I had not taken a course in International Finance, one of the key concentrations in International Economics, and simply decided to take a shot at it. Wrong! I had to wait another six months to bone up on that area and take the exams again. My factory labor/student mix continued while I studied for the exams and pondered what dissertation topic would best fit my course background and subject preference. In time, the exams were conquered, my dissertation topic selected and, after numerous exchanges of ideas, finally approved.

A dissertation is a serious project, amounting to in-depth research of a topic and months of thinking, writing, revising, battling with one's doctoral committee. With course work and exams completed, there was no reason to remain in Ann Arbor to work on the dissertation.

With a family, I had to find a job. That effort, along with choosing a location that would facilitate researching and writing up the dissertation, would take us of all places— a thrill just thinking about the move back East— to what we now lovingly call the Big Apple.

CHAPTER 7

A Doctor Should Fit the Mold

People don't usually think much about how doctors get where they are. Except for when we actually need them, doctors are a rarified breed, deeply embedded in the content of their medical expertise and how to implement it to good effect. Most people who have to deal with medical appointments do so without thinking twice about where doctors get their training, how long it took them to be certified, where they went for their internships or other practicum—and all the rest. In renowned hospitals we feel quite safe, but in many doctors' waiting rooms trust is often tested.

It's the same in Education and most other disciplines. In Education, students arrive at a college or university, line up their courses and time schedules, feeling satisfied if it all works out in practical terms. They seldom inquire about the professorial preparation the pillars of learning at the podium are presumed to have had. Students want faculty to be interesting, on time, kind, solicitous of their welfare in evaluating homework and grading tests. All of this is equally true when you take a car to the garage to solve a serious mechanical problem. We don't ask where the mechanics were trained and to how high a level.

That was the kind of thinking I did in taking advanced courses for my Ph.D. in Economics at the University of Michigan, followed by the enormous challenge of writing the infamous doctoral dissertation. Some call it "your book." I asked myself: will I be trained only in subjects the university and its professors deem essential to qualifying for the ultimate degree in my field, without consulting my own deeply -felt interests and goals? Many a candidate gets through years of course struggles only to flounder on the dissertation. For this reason, a significant number of doctoral candidates drop out sometime during that mind- stretching period of seeking an original topic to investigate. Or, having started on a subject area, they find that not enough meaty material is available to yield the doctoral level of sophistication needed to satisfy the seasoned and often skeptical dissertation committee of senior, highly credentialed but not always patient professors.

An academic doctoral dissertation is the climax and final step for career preparation. It's the point at the end of a long process where, at last, you can choose your subject for special in- depth examination. It's also the last daunting obstacle standing between the candidate and his most passionately desired goal: to become a full-fledged professor in a respectable college or university, or work in a prestigious company or other institutional environment. This calls for detailed research analysis of a subject area of *your* choice, where you have a challenge to convince people you can be a scholar in your general field as well as in specific subject matter of interest to *you*. It's not unlike a medical doctor, or any other specialist who must satisfy established experts in a field, so that he can legitimately be one of them.

When I came to this stage in my struggle for status in Economics, I asked myself this question: Confronting this long, grueling study I am about to prepare at the end of several years of concentrated course preparation, hundreds of hours spent listening to lectures, note-taking, studying, all the testing completed in each of perhaps thirty courses taken during undergraduate and graduate schools, all the research papers written, the horrendous investment of time, energy, stress, drive and anticipation of grade scores— after all this, should I not insist in my dissertation, my last chance to cap it all off, on choosing a subject and product content I embrace intellectually, philosophically and personally? I don't want to produce a book made up of stuff a committee has handed me to investigate, write up and defend. That can happen if you let it.

I want to feel that I have included important aspects of the field I've chosen to teach, explore and write about for years to come.

So, as a faith-based human being on the verge of posing as an expert, likely to be lecturing to and net-working with thousands of future peers and students, I asked myself: What have I neglected to cover ethically and philosophically in all my preparation to date? Enough of the side show of banal, sophomoric student attitudes, factory work, kitchen jobs, menial labor wage calculations and insecurities about surviving or getting ahead that make up a graduate student's mental and physical existence. I was about to shift gears into a more elite professional standing in the community of academics, and I wanted both to feel like and to be a competent scholar in my field but also a holistic person.

Pondering this momentous question, I came to this conclusion: With all of these years of grinding preparation and getting close to my ultimate professional credential, I had not yet dealt with how these student years would answer the core issues related to my beliefs, the precepts of my lifelong upbringing— the morality, rectitude, ideological foundations, the ethics of right and wrong of economic theory and life as it should be. These feelings and attitudes tie in with my more pedestrian and egalitarian view of our social fabric.

For these reasons, I rejected one of the standard approaches recommended for pursuing a doctoral dissertation along the more traveled road common in economics, where numbers are depended upon to establish a theory or case. You make the study a hard-nosed, statistical investigation. It is better, one is too often told, to take this route than wallow in the murky depths of subjective ideas, propositions and presumptions. True, you still have to orient whatever statistics you need as the basis of the thesis you've chosen to prove or disprove what you pose as logical conclusions. And vitally, you still have to find a subject that has not been examined thoroughly before by anybody else, whether it's statistical in essence or otherwise. Your doctoral dissertation has to be original and unique. If the statistics are available in the area you've selected and they can be manipulated in new ways to prove or disprove positions the public or the scholarly world had not yet known about, accepted or neglected to examine, you're still told that doctoral committees are less likely to find hidden subjective biases in statistics than in dissertations full of one's personal ideological beliefs. That's the dilemma I had to face.

I chose the subjective, philosophical, ideological route and then reworked my rationale for as long as it took to get my doctoral committee, comprised of economists, to accept my approach. I said to myself: I have come all this way without taking into account my faith and beliefs and how they relate to the subject field I have chosen to be my life's work; it was time for me to fess up and invite religion in. At least my conscience would be clear. I had no idea whether this proposal would pass muster with my doctoral committee. They could have rejected it outright, shot me down.

The title for my dissertation was "The Role of the Association of Catholic Trade Unionists in the American Labor Movement." I pulled no punches. It would be down- to- earth labor movement stuff that appealed to my sense of learning something about the social justice aspect of economics— a prime theme in the Catholic Church's Papal Encyclicals— about which up to now I knew precious little. However tough it might be to deal with the ethics, the morality, the prejudice issues, the matter of separation of church and state and more, I felt comfortable that my focus was right for me. I was facing up to the kind of professional economist I wanted to be: technically well trained, but broadly educated in the social aspects of economic theory.

Without being this explicit in my actual dissertation proposal to my Committee about my private motives, in substance the detailed coverage of my subject got me into such topics as the Catholic

Church's views on social justice in the work place, the comparative Influence of the Church on the Labor Movements of Europe and the United States, the Role of Catholic Trade Unionists in dealing with Communist, Socialist or Racketeering activity, how religion could function in trade union activity regarding such issues as wealth distribution, the fairness of wages, the politics of how government might deal with these matters—all this without infringing on matters of separation of church and state.

Would all of the activities of Catholic Trade Unionists be in harmony with personal rights of all unionists and with the Constitution of the United States?

Much of my thinking and preparation was underway before we left Ann Arbor for our new home on upper Broadway in New York, where we found an apartment across from Van Cortland Park, about a mile south of the Yonkers line. The commute to my first postgraduate job was but a few miles on the Cross Bronx Parkway to the Fordham University campus, where I would be an Assistant Professor of Economics. Any tenure consideration would, of course, be contingent on my completing my doctoral dissertation. Now with a family of two young boys in our midst, and a girl on the way, the task would be daunting, but compelling. I was determined to get it done no matter what. I had a beautiful wife who provided all the loving and competent support any man could wish for.

I was especially encouraged by the ample written evidence that there was a need for this study, and I quoted such sources. To give focus to my subject, I chose the work of a specific organization with structure, personnel and stated goals and objectives. *The Association of Catholic Trade Unionists* and their role in the American Labor Movement fit the bill. To validate my case as to why this study was worth conducting, I found useful, convincing evidence.

"I am amazed that no liberal journal has cared to follow the progress of the Association of Catholic Trade Unionists (ACTU)," one of them noted. "Nor has any magazine, to my knowledge examined the theoretical and practical principles of the Catholic Church as they relate to the labor movement. There is plenty to go on in the various papal encyclicals, in the history of labor in Germany, Italy and Spain since World War I, and in hundreds of local unions throughout the United States..." (James Higgins in the *New Republic* of March 7, 1949). Then there was the prominent authority on American labor history, Philip Taft, who said of ACTU that it was "a unique labor organization. It has grown in influence and today (1949) it is an important factor in a number of unions." An article in *Fortune* magazine back in those times said that this Trade Union group "achieved prominence in the United States labor scene." I flagged still more convincing and objective evidence support my choice of this organization and this topic as worthy of spending some years digging into its history, experience and influence in the American labor movement.

These testimonials and ten crowded bibliography pages displaying books, documents, pamphlets, articles, periodicals and other sources— including thirty personal interviews and letters— gradually gave me a lot of confidence in my choice of topic. They were key in getting the skeptical members of my doctoral committee to give me the go ahead. The interviews sent me scurrying about union offices and labor halls in the poor sections—even the notorious Bowery— of New York City, Detroit, Boston, Chicago, searching for the hands-on personal records I needed to put real life experience and opinions into the story. My confidence grew as I had a skein of valid information I could weave together to make a strong and practical case for producing a passable doctoral dissertation. That was critically important to keep up my morale because as I completed chapters and mailed them to Dr. Levinson, who chaired my doctoral committee in Ann Arbor, and then got them back with comments I could manage to incorporate in the text, I felt I was making progress. I was, at the same time, teaching a full load of Economics courses, both at Fordham in the Bronx and at night at the City Hall campus. With a wife and children to support, and another baby on the way, I was stretched to the limit, but making progress and always confident of ultimate success.

By the spring of the fifth year of this gritty, demanding work, forced by the committee to be tightly reasoned and supported by solid evidence and argument, I had completed "my book" of three hundred pages. I was prepared to travel to Ann Arbor in the spring of 1958 to defend my dissertation. My conclusions had defended this union organization's status and activity at the highest level of academic testing at one of America's premier universities. The following were accepted as proven by my inquiries, sources and analyses. Namely, that:

— the Catholic Church in this country encouraged workers to join and function within the typical non-sectarian union movement of this country.

— ACTU did not try to divert Catholic unionists toward the vagaries of utopianism as Socialists or Communists were wont to do.

— In its activities, principles and goals ACTU did *not* manifest religious bias when such issues arose among those of differing religious persuasion.

— ACTU members were not schooled in teaching religion, guided by the Vatican, or engaged in converting their fellow worker non-members.

— ACTU did not seek to put Catholics in positions of control in unions, but only those of acceptable ethical standards, as well as those not prone to racketeering behavior.

— ACTU's social policies, taken from Church documents, in fact, even antedated the famous Wagner Act of 1935 by nearly half a century, with the famed encyclical *Rerum Novarum* of Pope Leo XIII.

— ACTU's assistance to unions in general in organizing labor was demonstrated to be greatly appreciated by the leadership of unions involved.

The ACTU organization also grew apace from the late 1930's through the 1940's and '50's, with new chapters and sponsored newspapers appearing in many areas of the country in an era of much unrest and confusion. This supported the conclusion that there was clear evidence of a need for such an organization.

I have always felt that my dedication to this philosophical/ethical approach that capped my educational preparation for a life career— ostensibly oriented toward academe— profoundly influenced my intuitive decision-making in all of my subsequent professional positions, whether in teaching, government or business. And I attribute whatever successes I have experienced, through a long personal and professional life since graduate school, to the integrity of that decision. This despite the potentially crippling obstacles that could have tripped me up when I introduced religion and the precepts of my life's faith into the grueling process of investigating and writing the doctoral dissertation. I truly believe that through the many exchanges with my doctoral committee members, I had also educated them about a subject they might never have encountered. That is a belief I retain, intuitively based on the favorable responses I received from members of the committee who judged my work. They encouraged me in my pursuit and found the results worthy of a Ph.D. in economics from the University of Michigan.

With the Ph.D. parchment tucked under my arm— feeling so good inside— I called ahead to tell my spouse and kids that daddy had achieved what had at times seemed the impossible. I went home to the Bronx apartment and announced that to accommodate our growing numbers; we would now look for our dream house in the more bucolic environs of outer Long Island. Our lives would change for the better.

Chapter 8

The Yard Work Pants Return— But Not For Long

Living in Ann Arbor those several years took me out of garden work almost completely; I missed it, because I was brought up in it and often proudly raised my proverbial green thumb when a planting question arose. My life there was tied up with getting to classes, my academic work correcting papers, and especially the night shift at Willow Run. Likewise in New York. I had neither time nor the land in the crowded Bronx for planting vegetables and my favorite flowers. But getting out in the country, the one-third acre that came with our first owned home and land in Commack, Long Island, opened up again an opportunity for messing around in the yard. To get the size house we wanted at the price we could afford called for driving far out on the Island. I was commuting to a job on Madison Avenue, where for two-plus years I had signed on with Caltex Oil Company at double my Fordham salary, which tied up most days during the week, except for evenings in summer and the week-ends. Having met the Chancellor of Long Island University at a seminar and been offered a professorship at the University's campus nearer my home, I fled from that horrendous two-hour daily commute to a twenty-minute jaunt to the University's C.W. Post campus. Later, I would be lured even from the rewards of teaching and administering a department at that idyllic campus to take on distant challenges and scenes that neither I nor the rest of the family dreamed of. For now, the rustic life of Commack was heaven for all of us.

On week ends, especially, I relished getting into my work pants; I had several varieties but not dungarees as they were not yet popular back in the late fifties. Walking briskly behind the lawnmower or cultivating a garden patch and planting a mix of vegetables and my favorite blossoms on my hands and knees— ah, this was life! I recommend it for everybody. Getting dirty in real soil I always found therapeutic. After making the furrows for seeds with the hoe, gently covering them with hand-sifted soil, looking back at alternate rows of Canterbury bells, carrots and Swiss chard, or a patch of cucumber and lettuce at the back end of the garden, I would then add some double-colored pansies around the rim of the whole scene. My heart and soul were revived and recharged with feelings of connection to origins: gardening places, short commutes, income-earning and hard-thinking and worrying— the mix all in proper perspective.

Wiping the sweat from my brow, the hot rays of the noon-day sun burning down, the stiff knees and back strains entering my consciousness, I heard my wife's sweet voice calling me to lunch on the cool, screened-in porch at the back of the house: "Come, honey, and have a cold drink of lemonade and some lunch. You've been out there long enough!" True happiness enters our lives at times like these, doing the simple tasks, responding to simple requests of tenderness and love.

In the 50's and 60's, Commack was basically a rural community. Open fields were everywhere; large farms within a few miles catered to the needs of thousands with tons of potatoes and other vegetables, animal foods, including the much-favored Long Island Duck. Much to the joy of our children, the beaches were a ten-minute drive away.

Our move from congested New York City was a journey back to nature, in many ways, especially after I exchanged the Madison Avenue job for the professorship on the Island. It was a savings of at least 12 hours, enabling me to devote that time to my personal and family life. It was like crossing the bridge to sanity. It was a genuine revival of my spirit and outlook on living the better life. More time for family, gardening, neighbors, town activities, for trips about the Islands, cruising on the Stoneybrook Ferry North to Bridgeport, thence to Massachusetts and Maine to visit parents, relatives, and friends--all very uplifting to one's human spirit.

We also found ourselves buying different clothing for kids because they got into more outdoor games in the country: baseball, soccer, basketball, football tackles and the like. The laundry basket filled up every week with dirty shirts, pants, socks, even sneakers; they all put the washing machine to the test. For obvious reasons, washing machines out in the country became part of the standard offering in new homes in the distant suburbs and were much larger than the one we had in the New York apartment.

All of those heavenly days were about to come to a halt when I returned from a convention and announced that economists were in great demand for Foreign Service work. The subject and themes of my doctoral dissertation came into play. Standing in the convention hallway in New York, I stared at the six-foot poster: "FOREIGN SERVICE JOBS AVAILABLE." It stopped me cold. Top salaries, exotic travel, excellent housing, American and international schools, fulfilling professional opportunities for advancement. It was all about serving as an economist in the poorer countries of the world, and it struck me that I was being called. It wasn't an emotional surge or anything like that; and I wasn't just thinking in evangelical or religious terms. It only seemed to be the right line of work to be doing: helping the poor of the poorest of the third world countries make a better life for themselves. As I gathered the information about this venture into the parts of the world we'd never experienced as a family, it made a lot of sense. My beloved Uncle Sam would send us all to some country struggling to come out of the dread and dregs of poverty and strife, where I would apply my economic theory, experience, plus the social justice themes of my dissertation to creating strategies of hope and improved welfare for those people.

This would be a drastic change in the lifestyle of my family. We would be living in a strange country very far from home, very far from relatives and friends, far from everything we took for granted in our daily lives. From a land of plenty, we would be living in a land of poverty and even some danger of political strife. It turned out we didn't ourselves live in poverty; Foreign Service folk were well set up in housing, help and amenities to minimize culture shock and to enable concentration on service to their hosts.

What clinched the family decision to embark on this adventure was the country the U.S. Agency for International Development chose for us to serve. It was Jordan— in the Holy Land! It seemed too prophetic to be happening. This was the third time now that jobs that opened up our lives, minds and lifestyles seem to reflect a link not just to my graduate preparation in economics, but more specifically to the ethical and social justice themes I had selected to study and the family embraced. The first job offer after graduate school was at Fordham University, a Catholic institution run by Jesuits, the more thoroughly intellectually-trained arm of the priesthood. The second job with Caltex Oil Corporation grounded me deeply into the quantitative aspect of economic work: preparing forecasts of future supplies and demands of various products, in this case petroleum. There was daily crunching of these numbers and correlating them over a span of years with Gross National Product and other variables, then plotting the data on charts and, finally, writing it all up for use by company executives at the home office and company offices around the world. They, in turn, created marketing strategies and policies from these reports. I published some of these methodologies in respected Economics journals to enhance my credibility—and, possibly, to lead to pay raises.

This exposure to the quantitative side of economic practice turned out to be perfect preparation for the job in Jordan and led into future efforts of working with the less developed countries in various parts of the world. It all seemed to fit a pattern of progress in my career that was preordained after I completed all of my graduate work at the University of Michigan. It prepared me well, specifically, for working up numbers related to strategies for improving the lives of the poor in Jordan. I felt in complete harmony with the subject area, content of the job description and what I was expected to do when I got there. I was well-prepared technically to take up the challenge.

Preparing for the trip and experience, our four youngsters, my wife and I had to take a half- dozen or so immunity shots. The kids were not happy with this but understood, at least vaguely, why it was needed. They also understood this was a big leap into a new world for them and they had only their loving parents to depend on for their safety and well-being for the next two years. The peer, school and familiar home-site supports would disappear. All this done and understood, the government flew us first class across the waters, a stop-over in Paris, and on across Eastern Europe to the Middle East, landing in Beirut and then in Jerusalem, in the small yet exotic and Western— especially British-oriented Hashemite Kingdom of Jordan.

For Cecilia and me, everything about this amazing episode in our lives seemed to be a logical extension of our educational preparation, our upbringing in faith, and our aspirations about the kind of experience we had hoped for our future and that of our children. The tenets and names embodied in our upbringing in Christian beliefs, the Jewish foundations of it all, came to life all around us. We visited and stayed overnight in Bethlehem , the birthplace of Jesus, got to Nazareth where He was brought up in the carpenter trade, to Jerusalem where so much of His life played out, the Garden of Gethsemane, where His agony began before his condemnation and crucifixion. We walked the lanes where He was said to have walked. We spent two years getting around the region, to Damascus where St. Paul's experience of conversion took place, to Mt Nebo, where Moses looked out on the "Promise Land," to Israel where Christian sites existed, to the Jordan River where Christ was baptized.

Feeling thoroughly comfortable in this environment once in Jordan, I studied the country's natural resource base: agriculture, potash, tourism, some minor manufacturing in textiles, shoes, beverage companies, and various color marble quarries. I soon identified the flawed structure of the overall economy: the huge imbalances in their government's budget and country's international trade accounts; its dependency on foreign aid to cover its domestic budget debt and the use of that foreign aid to pay for its excess of the cost of imports over what it earns for exports. These made up the true tale of the Jordanian government's struggle to improve their economy and raise living standards and job opportunities for its people.

It's on these issues that the economist writes and orchestrates his skills. And here is how I fulfilled my inner drives to apply my formal preparation and beliefs about the human condition to uplifting the poorer folk in the world. It was like a calling, like church in many ways. It was what I was supposed to be doing with my life. It was getting back to the "overall days" of my childhood and the memory of all the menial jobs I had had early on, and going through schools and colleges doing dishes or waiting on tables in restaurants to earn my meals, or working as a laborer in a factory on the night shift— even such jobs in graduate school after spending almost three years as an officer in the Navy in World War II. The orchestration showed itself when I presented my strategies to Jordanian government officials, as was expected by the U.S. Ambassador and his team. I showed colored-lined charts of how to close those two debt gaps in their government and trade budgets by increasing irrigation agriculture in a country with sparse rains yet with rivers coming into the country from the North. By increasing the take on tourism by building and fashioning good hotels for visitors to The Holy Land, increasing the production of potash by building a more modern plant, and inviting companies to build more plants and produce goods currently being imported— like beer, shoes, textiles, special fabrics— they could revive the flagging economy. The point was all of this would generate jobs and business revenues that could be taxed to increase government revenues. Those revenues, plus a careful scrutiny of government spending to eliminate unneeded outlays, would eventually close the government's deficit. The cutting of imports by producing goods, when feasible to do so, at home, and increasing exports of agricultural goods showing up in greater numbers from irrigated farm lands, increasing potash and marble and other exports—these steps would in time wipe out the trade deficit as well.

Jordanian planning officials, one of them with a Columbia University Ph.D. in Economics, were somewhat startled that my strategies aimed at eventually eliminating U.S. foreign aid to their country and building economic independence. They were startled because leaders of dependent countries tend to be suspicious of colonialism and therefore believe foreigners don't ever want to leave, because by making their country dependent on them for survival, the foreign power can demand political and military policies to that country beneficial to the foreign aid giver.

I took satisfaction in all this because I was thinking and working hard toward improving the lot of the poor of Jordan, while at the same time improving the chances for the government and people of Jordan to be self-sufficient and politically independent from a foreign country.

I also got to see first hand the work of faith-based organizations like Church World Services, Catholic Relief Services as well as CARE and the United Nations UNICEF and private charities feeding and lifting the survival burdens of hundreds of thousands of desperately poor refugees, created by the violence of war. It was as though my doctoral committee at the University of Michigan had directed me to take on Jordan and Economic Development work as a follow -up practicum for carrying out the social justice themes of my dissertation!

This was but the beginning of these sojourns into dealing with the poor of the world. Later, having moved back to America and Potomac, Maryland, and partly due to a "Distinguished Achievement Award" from the Jordan Mission, I would become, in 1965, Chief of Planning for the Bureau for Near East and South Asia in the State Department in Washington, D.C. From there, my field of applications in carrying out my mission took me to such Third World countries as India, Turkey, Egypt, Afghanistan, Bangladesh and Nepal. These depressed countries provided a crescendo of opportunities for me to apply and test concepts and models in search of development solutions to produce economic growth.

This past travel agenda long preceded my late onset dungaree life, so Dongari Killa and Fort George in India were not in my sights yet, or I would have made a point to get there. Visiting each of these countries as part of my duties, I was struck by the vivid scenes of obvious need: primitive levels of urban and rural poverty, huts for housing with no electricity, no running water, wretched sanitary conditions, streets and sidewalks the home base for the unemployed, and governmental inertia and incompetence in planning against and overcoming these evils. Western personnel entering these panoramas of want did not have to "find" work to do; the challenges to their training in foreign aid work were palpable and called out for remedy.

In my book, *The Palestine State: A Rational Approach, 1977,* based on a decade of direct and associated involvement in Middle East events, I designed a program for potential economic progress and harmony for that area. It was to be founded on the basis of a steady and promising projection of political and economic advances that had been generated and projected during the late 1950's and into the '60's when peace existed between Jordan and Israel and regional political opportunism was contained. It was A Camelot era. I visited all of the countries above named, including Afghanistan, where peace reigned and I saw signs of economic and political progress. However, the seeds of today's political and economic woes in these countries were planted in those years, when political ambitions and reactions got out of hand, especially between Israel and Jordan. The 1967 war between Israel and Nasser's Egypt set in motion drastic realignments and upheavals. The second massive exodus of Arabs from the West Bank took place (the first being when Israeli independence was declared in 1948, leading to a devastation such that wars bring). The emigration of hundreds of thousands of West Bank Arabs to Jordan, Lebanon and Syria changed the delicate balance of power between Muslim and non-Muslim populations in those countries, where before that war sharing of political power seemed to work well. That war produced Hamas in Jordan and Hezbollah in Syria and Lebanon, the more radical and activist political parties, which in turn produced a more belligerent, aggressive Israeli stance against these parties. Israel's victory in that war likely sowed the seeds of radical Muslim approaches, leading to Osama Ben Laden's disaffection and, prospectively, the creation of the Taliban and the so-called U.S. "War on Terror," which consumes us to this day.

After six years of engaging in-depth in this laboratory of Third World problems and efforts to improve lives, I sought to return to where Ph.D. people usually end up: teaching and working in a university. On the way to that search, I stubbed my toe and was lured temporarily by circumstance back into the money nexus. My four no- longer- kids were getting near college age and tuitions were looming on the horizon. I succumbed to the temptation and took a good- paying salary from a great company located in Washington— then Peat, Marwick, Mitchell & Co., now German owned. The interruption took five years, during which at least I was still dealing with the poor of the world; my economic consulting projects took me to Panama, Venezuela, San Salvador, back to Jordan twice for State Department and United Nations budget reviews, Iran, Turkey, Afghanistan and Egypt again. I had not left the laboratory, just found a private sector funder for my work— which happened to tack on a profit motive, PMM & Co., after all, being entrepreneurs.

Well satiated with my faith mission for the less developed lands and its inhabitants, I did eventually get back to university life and work, which took me and my family back closer to our roots. My hometown was Beverly, Massachusetts on the North Shore waters; Cecilia's was Lewiston, Maine, where we first met. We found our final niche in South Dartmouth, Massachusetts on Buzzards Bay, within a feasible drive to those roots. It's here that the rest of the dungaree story and my transformation journey began to play out.

CHAPTER 9

Children Nestle Around: The Good Life

When we arrived here in Southern New England in 1975 and began searching for our new home, Cecilia was based in Potomac, Maryland trying to sell our house there, while I was in South Dartmouth on Buzzards Bay trying to find a house everyone would be pleased with. When Cecilia traveled here to review my list, the Greek Revival gem we finally bought was not even available, i.e. not for sale. It was a drive-by discovery with a real estate agent. Still, moves were made pronto by Cecilia to correct my oversight. "Could we just ask them if we can see it?" With my salary I said, "Out of reach." But Cecilia fell in love with this home— end of story.

Negotiations took place, the area economy was in recession, and compromise was reached. For $95,000 we moved in. As a reflection of the madness of the rise in property values in the past thirty years, even accounting for inflation, the current capitalization of the property rose more than ten-fold in thirty years. I used letters because it looks less obscene than numbers. On the other hand, accounting for inflation over that period, just in college tuitions alone, together with the Federal and state tax take if sold, the capital gain bonus takes a big hit.

You'd gather from this that where we settled we had a fair-sized lawn and yard dimensions to deal with—just shy of an acre-and-a-half. Front center stood our one-hundred-and-fifty-year- old Greek Revival style house, recorded by historians to be "one of the best examples of the style in the village." It was built by Chester Smith, a whaling captain. He had been to sea for five years from 1845 to 1850 as Captain of the bark "Junius." Upon returning home from Indian Ocean locations in search of whales and high-value oriental cargo, he retired a rich man, bought this property and built this great house. In June 1866 he sold the place to Archaelus Baker for $3,300, who proceeded to add a fine carriage house to the property for horses, a barn which we in our time here rented out to the swallows every summer for decades, in exchange for watching them build six or seven nests, feed and launch 25 or 30 hatchlings annually, and in the process collectively devour many thousands of the hated mosquitoes around our property. When I learned that Captain Baker died the August after selling the estate, at age 51, I was determined *never* to sell the property in *June,* no matter what.

The size of the lawn to maintain I thought of as a conditioning issue. I bought a Sears riding mower and a small walking motorized mower to do the job. Exercise I consider essential for good health and long life; I have always been big on it—sports, gardening or any kind of yard work, chopping wood (the house has five fire places!), painting, digging holes for shrubs, filling pots and large ceramic planters with summer flowers and vines, trimming large bushes and trees. It's endless. Rather than use the riding mower, I used the manual walking mower— great for my arms, legs and shoulders. I spent my teen years doing estates, remember? Even when I did tire a little, rather than sit in the seat of the riding mower, I would walk along side and steer the machine. It kept me walking rather than sitting. The neighbors thought I was nuts, but I enjoyed and much valued this type of conditioning. At ease in my old clothes, I experienced the feeling and emotions of release from the weekly stretch of formal office work and exchanges with ambitious professionals in education and business.

Every form of conditioning is good for the body, mind and soul. When you are content with your physical wellness at whatever the age, it contributes to maintaining a positive attitude toward all aspects of a busy life—moving about with energy and purpose, thinking sharply, speaking confidently. Another conditioning activity came to my rescue from the age of fifty forward. All those great younger years in several sports, all the yard work around the three homes we have owned with lawns and gardens became a bonus for my tennis game. Steroids are in no way a sane substitute for the natural routes to body and mind conditioning.

A word or two about the tennis game. Given the sports of my youth, tennis was not a natural for me. I played because it was another game to try and enjoy. In Beverly Cove, public funding had built a tennis court five minutes from my house at the playground, and it was free—when you could get on. I swung the tennis racket using the same arm swing I would use pitching a baseball. The only difference was I also wound up in advance of serving the tennis ball, which, along with the muscle tone from my yard work, gave my serve a lot of zing. Much of the fun of tennis when over fifty is in teaming up in foursomes. We tried to match talent and temperament so as to optimize the competitive give and take and minimize the handicaps on both sides of the net. We had five in what we called our "Jolly Five": Frank, Dan, Mike, Cliff and I. To get the most benefit physically and mentally from the contest, you have to work at balancing the talent on each side of the net. This optimizes the competitive give and take of any doubles game. Mike and I played the usual amateur over-fifty game—tenacious, opportunistic, an occasional unexpected bullet down the alley, just out of the lunge of the opposing net man who had misread the moves and leaned toward center net. We were great "getters," as we stretched the full reach and strength of our late years to pick up the soft shot that just caught the outer edge of the line. Each of us made our share of foolish mistakes—whamming the easy one— swoosh!— into the net, hitting one too long or too short, thinking to prevent the return zinger that, instead, came right back between us. "Yours!" we yell at each other, eyes popping, the dead feet, dead racket end result as the ball sailed by us.

Frank was the better half of the other twosome. Unlike the rest of us, he'd had lessons for some years as a youngster, often, as he was quick to say, against his will. His father had hoped to make a pro out of him. Frank rebelled. In fact, he quit the game for ten years to show whose boss in the end. Now over fifty, he was back in full bore, very consistent—chalk some of it up to that early training—strong, far-reaching in covering his side of the court, accurate, terrific "get" man, powerful first serve, failing that, the soft second threw Mike or me off— and we blew it. Dan compensated for Frank's driving game: a little erratic, but got the ball back most of the time, able to hold his own— patience personified. His most punishing shot was a high lob that took so long to come down that either Mike or I were wound up like cork screws. So exasperated were we by the time the ball came down that our racket swing, tweaked by our irritation, and was so wild that the ball sailed off at high speed toward the ceiling or over the back or side net of the court. We called those lobs being "lobotomized" by Frank.

Usually on the court beside us a women's rotating group brightened up the scene every week with colorful tennis dress, high-pitched responses during play, less intensity when play went awry. These were Cecilia's partners— mothers all. As the Jolly Five's game ended before theirs, we had time to sit and observe through the window of the indoor tennis court waiting room. We noticed their more looping ball play compared to our hard strokes and smashing overheads. Some women had muscled arms— derived, we assumed, from gardening, housework or their group exercise exertions— all good body and mind conditioning. Others showed softer, more slender arms. The whole scene was very feminine and appealing to us as we watched. There was a more relaxed pace to their game, more ladylike approaches and swings at the balls. Yet, their game was very competitive, even though much less ruckus going on about bad or good calls.

When the young ones in the family had hit their late teens the dynamics of family life had changed. Each of our four had graduated from Potomac High School in Maryland and colleges became the big priority. Where to go? While Cecilia and I as parents believed that the final choice should be with Tim, Rich jr., Mary and Chris, still we did some fairly heavy leaning in terms of criteria. Tim and Rich were the first in line to do the college tour routine. We said, O.K. But! I ranted some— well I'll admit, too much.

"Look. Let's not spend time on colleges or universities nobody ever heard of. They may be fine— their campuses or their sports complex may appeal to you, a friend of yours is going there, and on and on. But if nobody ever heard of it, you will spend the rest of your life answering a series of bothersome questions from people: What did you say the name of it was? Where did you say it was? What kind of special academic programs? Does it have any sports teams anybody ever heard of? What made you pick that school? Your best friend going there or something? Pick some place that is known. They come in all sizes and programs and locations. There are high quality small colleges and high quality big universities; the high quality ones tend to be popular. There are some very good and well known Catholic colleges and universities that come in every size.

"The advantages of the quality, widely-known college and university syndrome— as you get your degree there, and as you live your life afterwards— is that you don't have to be answering those annoying questions the rest of your life. Instead of friends saying "Huh?" when you tell them where you're going, they nod their heads in the affirmative because they know instantly what place you're talking about. They may not know any specifics about academic programs or about the performance of your sport teams at least they know your school is well known from having seen it named on TV sports news or games and such, and that for most people is enough for them to assume the school is a good one. Whether that's a reasonable conclusion or not is irrelevant, as long as you and we as family know the quality aspects of the college or university.

"The other thing is where this place is? You don't want Alaska, North Dakota, Texas, Arizona, Florida, Wisconsin—such places; hey, we'd never see you except maybe twice a year. Would you really want that distance from everybody? Think about it. Get a decent distance away from home— absolutely but don't exile yourself from all you know and have known for months, missing birthday gatherings, parental anniversaries , a grandparent's or old neighbor friend's funeral, and the like. It isn't worth it. It's not wrong to choose the long distance. In fact it may in the long run serve a better purpose in building independence from family emotions and distractions. Yet, is it really worth it in this short life?"

That was my advice— an old duffer's shtick. Yet, I think we are a closer, more loving family because of the bonding of that nearness during all those undergraduate and graduate college/university years. Could I be wrong on all this? Do I have the evidence in some detail to support this advice? Yes, to question one; no, to question two. Countless thousands of college student opinions, if recorded somewhere, could prove a confirming contrary opinion.

Anyway, slice it as you will, that's a lot of directive vibes to pass on to teenage offspring trying to mature and make their own choices about important steps in their lives. But, if after listening to all this they came up with a strong, rational case for a totally different alternative, we would listen and advise and maybe even agree with a smile and full support. Maybe.

By naming a few schools we thought plausible to fit our pitch, no doubt it made it pretty hard for our college-bound wonders to be contrary about this advice. For example, we had mentioned Villanova, Georgetown and Boston College because they were quality Catholic colleges. As we were living in Potomac when Tim and Rich went off first to college, we took them to see Villanova in Pennsylvania— Tim first, Rich the next year. It was a well-known university with quality degree disciplines, plus graduate schools, including a law school. It's sports programs were nationally publicized on TV and radio. As we planned our move to New England, Mary and Chris toured the Boston area, including Boston College and Newton College of the Sacred Heart. Chris favored B.C. and Mary liked Newton, and that's where they went. Later, Newton College merged with B.C. and adopted its name (which solved the "well-known" criteria I ranted about). They liked everything about the campuses and programs they viewed, and being near Boston with all of its cultural offerings but a few minutes away on the public transit systems was huge plus.

Both Villanova and Boston College were just right: They were high-quality schools with prominent graduate offerings; they were nationally known; they were away from home, but within easy reach of family events and friends. Villanova was a jaunt from our new home in S. Dartmouth, Mass., but it was no long day's journey into night, for heaven's sake.

As time passed and each graduated from college and some went on to professional schools of law , communications and real estate brokering, and each thereafter practiced their professions— three in Massachusetts and one in New Hampshire— we felt blessed. All four married, nestled not too far from us here in New England and, while one has moved back to the Virginia area after a nine year geographic proximity, we enjoyed the good life. Grandkids soon came onto the scene—eight of them ultimately— and all gather at the homestead to celebrate all those occasions family engage in throughout each year. In the yard, we played touch football, softball, whiffle ball, many other pick up games together. We gathered in the fall to rake up about 100 bags of the fallen leaves, each of us wearing a yellow sweater that read: "Grandpa's Leaf Posse"— the sewing handiwork genius of our beloved, creative daughter Mary, nifty artist in her own right. We had some gatherings of nieces, nephews and their parents, including upwards of fifty of us for the massive barbecue celebration of a special anniversary.

All of the above reminisces dealing with our offspring, the settling into new homes and caretaking of home and yard and of one's body and mind through lots of physical activity, including tennis, was part of the good life. It took us through the decades of those middle and upper middle years of our lives when adults are the most committed to hard work and ambition in their professions. We dealt with the stress, with the joys of yard and garden work and play, in which we all share. It kept us feeling young, even perhaps all too invincible.

Especially when things go right and tragedies and true hardships, by the grace of God you have to say are avoided, it is hard to imagine endings of the wonderful years that pass by in the lives of families.

The span of time for us as a bonded unit was so active, so full of good times and features and good fortune for all of us, so prolonged through the decades even unto old age, that interruption of the peace seemed impossible. Yet such abrupt upset of the routine can happen and does when any member of a loving family relationship passes from the halcyon scene.

CHAPTER 10
A Death in the Family Tolls Many Bells

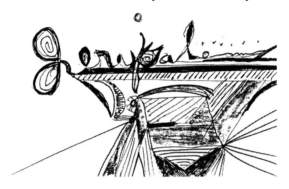

The good life does not have to end with the loss of a member of the family, yet a very profound change takes place. The bells tolled and reverberated through the immediate family and in the different ways that she touched people everywhere. When my beloved Cecilia left the scene forever, they chimed sadly for my offspring who had in abrupt fashion lost the deep earthly love and wise, gentle, devoted guidance of their mother. They reverberated for our relatives scattered about the country who saw in her the essence of gracious concern and involvement in their well-being with her open arms and bright, enabling smile and ever-eager welcomes to family gatherings and celebrations in our home. Those bells pealed for her countless women friends who highly valued her love and kindness, the brilliance of her conversation and observations, even when blindness came, and in gatherings when presiding over their club planning and activities. They resounded among her professional colleagues, who from her work would recall her intelligence and skill in promoting programs for the University of Massachusetts Dartmouth, as well as for businesses in their products and community outreach projects, using her writing and editorial wizardry to publish newsletters and other copy and, with her beautiful dulcet voice—honed with years of experience in radio—speaking in public forums. They rang out in the minds of neighbors and strangers alike, wherever— whether in the United States or abroad or alive or aloft with God—and in whatever status she met them, from King Hussein of Jordan, ambassadors, U.S. senators, military generals, wives of Secretaries of State, university presidents or professors and unto the lowest of the poor and peasant, who each recognized as soon as she spoke, the special nature, ingratiating manner and presence of this exceptional woman, my treasured wife of fifty-five years.

In the lives of all these folks, a bell was heard, quietly perhaps, but clear in the depth of memory or ethereal awareness of each, when they learned of the death of Cecilia. I'm convinced that they felt the absence of her compelling spirit.

She had struggled through all of that good life I just described with insulin-dependent diabetes, as part of her daily life for forty-two years. You would not have detected it in her demeanor or behavior from how much we enjoyed our later years. While treating the disease became a normal daily routine those many years—testing her sugar count and injecting insulin four times a day —her personality or disposition never changed. She remained serene and confident as a mother, a professional woman, a warm and fun-loving spouse. She proved to the family and all her friends that even without good health, you can function normally in the home, dealing with a growing family of four, and with the professional demands of a job. She shied away from nothing. She took on roles that you might expect her to avoid as a drain on her health. Until the loss of her eyesight after thirty-seven years of the disease, she engaged in projects and challenges as though nothing had changed her life, even doing book reviews. Whatever she was asked to do for the University, in her job or for community organizations, she thought of herself confidently as the woman for the task at hand.

Throughout the five years of her life in blindness, Cecilia seldom complained. She accepted her trial philosophically as part of life's turns— that it was meant to be. She was a woman of deep faith in her Catholic upbringing and education. An honor student and top debater at her high school and at Trinity College in Washington D.C., where she excelled in academics, drama and leadership roles, awarded the "Trinity Pin," the highest honor it bestows on the outstanding graduating student.

She moved about as an elderly woman with grace and purpose in that, in her perception, it was God's will for her. It was a lot to expect her constitution to manage forever, so many years of damage, not only to her eyes but, more troublesome, to her vascular system and her heart. Just a month short of her eightieth birthday, on June 19, 2006, she died suddenly in my arms at 2 a.m. from a heart attack.

We often introduce our wives, perhaps in a joking or condescending tone, as "my better half."

I did not realize how true that was until she left my side after fifty-five years of wedded bliss. Yet, it was important not to let that change my natural optimism about life, as it would impact family, relatives and friends. She left a beautiful statement behind in her desk, perhaps years ago, in anticipation of her death, that she was now happy in a better place and wanted me to be happy too, though left behind without her. It has not been easy, as so much of our personal lives meshed in so many ways— in personal intimacy, socially, in the books we read together, in our travels to the Middle East, England, France, to professional conventions or on assignment in Hawaii, San Diego, St. Louis, the Bahamas, New Orleans, Seattle, Montreal, Ireland, Madrid, Italy, Florida. We were and remained as one, in conformity with the preachments in the wedding ceremony five and more decades earlier. My love for her will never die.

Though retired for ten years when she died, I was always busy with writing, serving on University of Massachusetts committees, Co-Founder and President of its Retirement Association, Community Boards of Directors, the downtown Business Luncheon Club. I am involved in our Parish Church functions, in the Movie Club I had started for her in our home, so that she could reciprocate invitations she received on a regular basis from her friends. This way, she could sit near the TV set and get glimpses of the action going on, while playing host to her friends. That movie club has become a regular, using Netflix, ever since, enabling me to continue a tradition geared initially for her need. Her friends always loved to come to our house, and now can still enjoy the ambience. They bring goodies and drinks to help out the bachelor in residence. The companionship and sociability of that event, offered every other week or so, that served her so well is now serving me, as well as her friends who attend. It keeps me connected to the life we had.

As part of the grieving process, I spent a year-and-half, following her death, writing a biography of her life. That kept her around a little longer in my presence. I started two other books, one about Malta for a woman who showed me a fascinating diary of a nurse who had served in World War II on that beleaguered Island. It was bombed daily for several years by German and Italian air raids, leaving that small, historic place in ruins. I was asked if this diary was worth publishing; it certainly was and is. Doing the research and supplementing the information for that project also occupied some of the quiet hours in the years after Cecilia's passing. "Nursing during the Siege of Malta" will appear in good time.

I continue to write regularly, as with this manuscript. Yet, despite all the various activities I pursue and the legion of personal and professional friends interacting with me, it's essential for me or anyone whatever the age, not to be overly idle. Keeping mentally and physically active keeps the body and neurons stimulated, alive and responsive. Busy as I always seem to be, there is never enough new creative involvement to fill those many lonely hours.

I began to spend more time and became more cognizant of the spiritual part of grieving and what was expected in the way of coping. The literature on this phenomenon, I learned, was prolific. I explored and became more aware, through reading and Church faith and bible study seminars, of the role of suffering in one's path to "salvation" in the Christian tradition. Suffering is not a popular subject for human beings. We know it goes on all around us and all around the world, yet who wants to dwell on it? Nobody. But how much delving into it are we supposed to do? For how much of it are we ourselves responsible? When you lose a spouse, if in no other instance, you discover what true suffering is. It is stressful and it hurts, physically and mentally. It is a goad to life transformation.

It doesn't take much listening or reading to know that the world is full of innocent suffering and deliberately inflicted suffering. Innocent suffering victimizes people who are not responsible for it: The Holocausts of history, the genocides, civilian victims of the ravages of war, earthquakes, floods of rivers, ocean tsunamis, epidemics of various diseases, and acts of terrorism like September 11, the starvations in Dafur. The list goes on. Some are inflicted deliberately by man, some are nature's wrath. Victims in these cases are innocent sufferers. We are obliged to help these millions of sufferers when we can.

The issue of grieving gets pretty personal, almost unavoidably, and each of us deals with it in very private ways. From the beliefs we inherited and fostered in our family, there is the suffering of Jesus Christ who saw it coming, but did not seek to avoid it.* He didn't resist the authorities and political powers that condemned, tortured and crucified Him. In our Christian belief, He was assigned by God the Father to do this to redeem mankind. The difference between his suffering and ours, according to our belief, is that because he was Himself sinless, he was innocent. We are not. We humans carry original sin with us; basically it means that we are prone to do wrong things and must constantly battle against those leanings.

The bottom line for me in handling the loss of my spouse is that without suffering we cannot atone for our sins. Atonement is repairing our broken relationship with God for our earthly offenses against His commandments, so that we can gain salvation after death: we get our ticket to the eternal Paradise. This may seem far adrift from our story line, but actually ties in with my finding diversions to soften the stresses of coping with a death in the family, one of them leading me, strange as it may seem, into the dungaree world and transforming soul searching.

---

*My understanding of Suffering benefited from John E. Theil's, *God, Evil, and Innocent Suffering,* The Crossroads Publishing Company, New York, 2002.

So, while I have accepted the onerous chore of having to suffer some, I work hard to minimize it. I eagerly seek diversions— social and entertainment activities, lots of contact with others in and outside of my professional interests. In my need to be newly creative and always busy with some additional constructive work, I started to probe my file cabinet. I began by disposing of everything I thought irrelevant to my future or any family member's well being. I came upon a large folder of sheets and half-sheets, scraps of paper—well over a hundred of them— packed together. There were doodles on all of them, collected, as I said earlier, from the long past at graduate school on down to the present. I was about to cast them all into the trash bag I was using to empty my files of useless records of all kinds, connected to past jobs and interests no longer pursued.

The doodle project was thus linked to the loss of Cecilia, as I labored over them for diversion.

I have come full circle to the origins of this convoluted dungaree tale. Finally, I took that folder of doodles out of my file cabinet and began to wonder what to do with them. Having made the decision to go public with them, I still had to get into the dungaree style of living, at least while I was working and socializing with the artists at Gallery X. The fateful meeting with those artists has led me to buying a pair of jeans and a pair of dungarees— ostensibly, at eighty- seven years of age, my last dungarees. But, to repeat, must they be my last?

Chapter 11

Jeans, Dungarees or Watchamacallit?

First, I've got to get this off my chest. I mean for a man like myself in his eighties, using the dungaree as a source of transformation, it is no cake walk to enter the loaded isles of pants in a department store aiming to buy jeans or dungarees that you expect to match your mind set. This is how it went.

I stroll toward the men's section where pants are sold. Specifically, I'm looking for dungarees, the working jean with its extra pockets and loops for tools. I find them piled up on tables and shelves. I also find jeans. I'm looking for someone who's knowledgeable about the subject, because I'm confused. I don't want to waste my time talking to somebody who just sells 'em but doesn't know the difference between jeans and dungarees. So, I'm stopped and gazing around to find somebody who looks like a supervisor.

Ah, that woman might be in charge of this section.

"Mam." She looks up from the clothes she is folding. "Could you tell me the difference between jeans and dungarees?" While she was thinking of an answer, I was thinking of overalls and the practical uses of all that genre of clothing that figures in ordinary lives almost everywhere, with little of the philosophical connection I later discovered.

I grew up wearing "overalls" which covered the clothes you didn't want to get dirty that you had on underneath the overalls. They are still popular almost everywhere: In farm country— especially Midwest or farther West, where ranchers and farmers swear by them. They are popular also among railroad workers. After all, working at dirty yard or dusty rail beds all day could mess up your good work clothes underneath, or the long johns or union suits some men wore. Overalls can slip over everything and just be easily taken off before washing up and sitting down to eat a meal in the clean garb worn underneath. There's the so-called "boiler suits" for guys who work around coal-fired boilers, usually called "Coveralls." It's a one-piece affair but has long sleeves and looser, jumpsuit-like legs. Americans were the first to use overalls in a version of a military uniform as far back as Revolutionary War days, part of regulation wear for some of the militia units. Currently, the U.S. Navy assigns a dark blue coverall as a working uniform, with "U.S. Navy" on the chest of the suit and rank insignia on the points of the collar. In the Second World War and subsequent battles, black, khaki or olive drab coveralls were and are everywhere, including Iraq; the drab is worn by armored tank or truck personnel. Strange as it may seem, car and drag racing drivers also use coveralls. Construction workers are overall users. It's sometimes referred to as a "bib-and brace" overall, with trousers and a front patch covering the chest and suspenders to hold them up.

Can't forget the flash of new-style bib overalls that popped up in the *avant garde* 60's; young people of both sexes wore them in different colors and fabric patterns, sometimes with one of the straps worn loose or unhitched, hung along the side or under the arm. I wouldn't know, but I'm told some rock entertainers, too, wear coveralls in their public concerts.

So you see, even in affluent America, where you might have thought the old "overall" of my youth and salad days had all but disappeared, 'tain't so. It's still out there, very prevalent and useful, even colorful.

But the U.S. isn't the only part of the world that got into overalls. Along with patriots, even British loyalist military units during the Revolutionary War— mostly infantry soldiers all— slouched around in these get-ups to protect the pants and stockings they wore underneath, although it wasn't long before the overall was officially issued to replace the pants, especially in the summer months of that Great War. Our Canadian neighbors have been into overalls, too, for farmers and as a coverall field uniform in WWII, mostly khaki but also black and green; they were worn both at home in Canada and in Germany during and after the war, while carrying out training exercises as armored and mechanized units. My sources tell me that "student overalls"—actually coveralls—are donned in Scandinavian countries to convey a "party-uniform" image, with insignia on the back and colors to represent the cause or university, suggestive of U.S. students of the sixties.

I had to clear my memory of all that irrelevant information, 'cause it was how doodles and dungarees, the working jean, came together in the artist's Gallery X that was on my mind.

Finally, the store clerk said, "There's no difference between jeans and dungarees. Everybody used to call them just "Levis"; they're just the same, really."

Well, even before I came into this store I had heard differently about that. So, this woman was no supervisor. So, I'm peering around over the tops of the tables piled up with denim pants of various kinds— blue, beige— looking for a supervisor.

Ah, there he is. "Sir, can you help me out?" He smiles nodding, "Yes, what do ya need?"

"What's the difference between jeans and dungarees?"

"Not much," he says

Oh God— he's no help either. "I was told that the dungaree was a working pant and had cloth loops for holding tools like a hammer or a folding ruler, like construction workers use. Also extra pockets for other things. See, I'm working on a book, and I'd like to get this straight."

"A book! " He looked directly at me for the first time; I got his attention.

"Well, yes," he says, "some jeans or dungarees have those." He showed me some jeans with loops. "See, holding up a pair— these jeans have loops for tools, just like dungarees."

"Yeah, I see that." Some consternation with this unexpected revelation. Still, I'm thinking stylish jeans don't have loops.

Assuming I was satisfied that he had filled me in on a lot I had to know, he hurried off the scene, down the corridor. He wasn't about to take a chance on my finding, while examining shelves of Levis and Arizona or Lee Brands, that he made a mistake.

I got into pulling pants off the shelves, running into all kinds of descriptions: Levis, "boot cut jeans" to accommodate high-heel shoes or boots; Arizona's big side pocket "cargo" jeans. These were mostly beige in color, rather than the typical light or darker blue; "sneaker fat" jeans-you can guess that one; silvertabs' "baggy fit", and that one too; "skinny jean" speaks for itself; Lee's "relaxed straight or crooked Leg"— that one beats me. There is also a "regular" jean, which is a tighter leg and thigh fit and a "relaxed fit" jean—slightly less tight around the waist and legs.

By this time, I was more confused on definitions of jeans and dungarees than before I came into this store. Overalls, I understood from my boyhood, but this mix left me dazed.

After rummaging through stacks of jeans and dungarees and different brands for about twenty minutes, I think I came up with, for me, a workable answer, as follows:

All dungarees are basically "carpenter" pants— meaning that they have loops or small side or back pockets for holding construction or carpenter-like tools or perhaps even measuring tapes. There is an Arizona brand carpenter dungaree and a Lee carpenter dungaree. There is also a so- called "original" jean, which is not a carpenter pant, but a jean with no extra loops or extra side or thigh pockets for carpenter tools. That's the one that gets most of the style play.

Having struggled through this, I came out of the store with a pair of Lees brand "relaxed fit," "original" darker blue jeans (with no loops or pockets), and a pair of Lees brand lighter denim "carpenter" dungarees with a loop for a tool on one side and a small extra thigh pocket on the other side. The Lees brand "relaxed fit" jean I wear to Gallery X meetings, feeling much at home, now, with my new-found colleagues. I've taken notice of the fact that so many older people wear jeans more commonly to informal activities, like trips to the library, to spontaneous invites to lunch with friends at a Chinese or pizza restaurants, or on their daily errands to grocery stores, pharmacies or other errands. I wear mine now occasionally when out in the evenings to a cabaret-style café where a small music group with guitars, violins, flutes is performing Celtic ballads or similar mood melodies. In my retirement years, it's a new look I've cultivated for the informal entertainment or gallery hours I attend, just to match the times and sell my doodles. A phase of the transforming process is underway.

The "carpenter" dungarees are a heavier fabric, hence warmer, but also less dressy, yet very acceptable for around the house or out doing chores.

How often in history do the affluent in society copy in public the clothing styles of a lower social class? Well, it's a big world out there, but if the research was complete on this issue, the answer would likely be— not often. You can say it has happened in the contemporary world we live in. The evidence is everywhere. Once the working man's garb, denim jeans and dungarees, cargo pants and all the rest crossed the line decades ago, up into the preferred styling choice of the upper classes of our society. Even at the country's most expensive—even quite elite—private schools and high-cost universities, the store-bought pants come with poor- man patches sewed into the knees or seductively onto a cheek of the rear end. If I were learned in the fabric business, knew all the marketing niches and statistics on customer penetration, I could add several more pages to this testimony about how the choice dress styles of the rich and the elite in late 20th century and early 21st have absorbed, with relish, the dress codes of the economically less fortunate of our world.

I have discovered another period in history when a comparable twist of attitudes about clothing styles happened. In the mid and latter years of the 18th century, expressions of regret were common about the poor no longer spinning their own clothes but buying them in shops. No less a figure than Voltaire, the affluent French philosopher, author and towering intellectual genius, weighed in on this subject. He saw maids and farm girls in fancy gowns cavorting about and young, lower class men in high fashion on horseback in the public parks.

Actually, it went both ways. Styles between the classes, it was said, varied very little.

Wealthy women were wearing aprons of maids, and servant girls were wearing pricy silk scarves. Working men and the elite alike were wearing seaman's jackets and expensive pants and shoes. What's going on here?

Easy to see how the elite bought the clothing styles of the poor. But how, you ask, could the poor buy the clothing of the rich? It was a feature of the marketing, credit and social systems of the time. The poor bought on credit, "running up debts as high as their annual income…to shopkeepers and employers." Then there were the markets and country fairs, both flooded with smuggled and stolen goods, sold cheap in second hand shops to the resourceful and style conscious poor. Manufacturers of clothing of all kinds often miscalculated market trends and overproduced, then proceeded to dump their surpluses onto the shopkeepers, fairs and other clothing outlets. Poor people found a way. Rich people, for their part, succumbed to the exotic allure of imitating the poor; they went "plebian style."

Back then, it was a revolutionary two-way switch in dress between rich and poor and, more to our story here, it foreshadowed the contemporary massive surge of denim jeans and dungarees, once worn only be cowboys and French workmen from Nimes!*

So, I am but a speck in the new style revolution, but into the denim world I came. And into the modern shopping malls did I plunge to indulge in the "plebian" rage.

I haven't lost my identity in all this. Yet I have the feeling I have discovered a new me inside that has found expression. I still go to the Symphony, to shows in Boston, to lectures of interest, to the Luncheon Club with my peers. I'm still the retired academic with official assignments on Boards and committees which meet on serious business (mostly fund-raising). For these occasions, I slip back into my more formal garb—jacket, ties, gray slacks, matching sleeveless sweaters. I look nice, but official. Yet I am changed. Is this a benevolent form of Jekyll and Hyde split-personality syndrome I've acquired, or just a more open expression of my hitherto restrained right-brain life? What is this new me? That calls for some explanation.

*Indebted for 18th century knowledge to Ferdinand Mount in his review of John Styles' book, *The Dress of The People*, Yale University Press, in his article "Cherryderry Days", *The Times Literary Supplement*, April, 2008, p.3.

CHAPTER 12

Doodles, Dungarees and New Beginnings

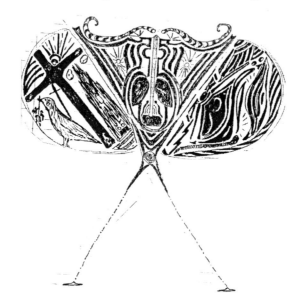

The overalls from my youth and dungarees of my senior years are symbolic of the changes I have undergone, through the menial labors and youthful play games of early days, to a long, satisfyingly varied and successful professional career, finally to revived expressions of art, culture and spirituality.   Most of life is spent struggling for status and security by building educational or training foundations to achieve personal goals. The more analytical and objective left brain was kept busy. The right-brain subjective, intuitive, visual me was there in my doodles, but much less expressed otherwise.   For me, life has meant establishing goals and work environments that match beliefs and social values. That's likely what most of us try to do, some deliberately, some by sheer accident or happenstance.   It then becomes the daily chore of living out those values day by day, and doing what you are expected to do well.

My values, in my perception, were fairly conventional, but essential to finding inner contentment and ambition to achieve. A cherished wife with shared values was at the inner core of that contentment and projection of my hopes for the future. Building a family and visioning the future of children was crucial in our joined feelings, projected into hopes and plans. Once well-educated, I worked at achieving the American dream—the material attributes of professional success: a home in the right setting for parents and kids, good neighbors, cars for the working couple, family travel opportunities, educational quality for our offspring.

To achieve enduring individual and family contentment, longevity is essential. We have been blessed, Cecilia and I, with long lives. The latter years have been about as exciting as any family could want to experience, because we were around to do things, go places, achieve our goals in life and watch our children achieve theirs. Our offspring have been the pride and supreme pleasure of our lives. All four now in their fifties, we have had the joy of communicating with them on personal, family, as well as their professional expectations, concerns and obstacles, and have been able to participate in their journeys toward new beginnings. How my life and longevity could be anything but enriched and blessed by such a tribe!

This is the thing about being healthy and living long. A long life gives you much more time not just to achieve goals but also to enjoy your family's activities, their growing into adulthood, their personalities, their boisterous gatherings, all before your health declines and your mind loses its sharpness. We all know how accidents, early fatalities, health set-backs can wreak havoc on plans for the idyllic life, because it takes a long time to build up to that life you imagined in your plans for the future. Priorities and plans are crushed by detours to cope with destructive forces. It may sound simple and obvious but to achieve a reasonably long life takes some work. True, good inherited genes are an excellent beginning to the path of a long life. Given this, though, you have to give your genes and your lungs a chance to help by eating right and breathing right.

I am neither a nutritional specialist nor an MD. In fact, you can put me down as a dilettante about it. But, eating right means three balanced meals a day—as my mother always insisted— giving the body make-up and chemistry a chance to serve in this process. You don't need to have a resident nutritionist in the house to eat balanced meals. Moderation in everything: meats, fish, vegetables (green, yellow, brown), eggs, fruits, potatoes, milk, cheese, water, desserts. Again, each and all in moderation, but every day, some combination of these. Such ingredients can be prepared, cooked and embellished in various ways and forms. And there are ample substitutes that maintain the essentials for the body.

Eating right feeds and builds good physical condition; it feeds the mind and the spirit with well-being. You can get away with eating the wrong foods for a long time, especially when young.

Eventually, a steady diet of only one type of food— starches, meats, processed foods, so-called junk food (name your own) will undermine the body's wellness, and in turn diminish mental acuity and, I believe, even more vitally that later time in life when so many good things you worked for can be enjoyed.

Now, the next vital thing: breathing. What do I mean by that? Well, it pertains simply to the lungs. You want good, strong air passages into the body to the lungs and diaphragm. It requires fresh, not dirty air. Fresh air to the lungs and diaphragm is stimulus to the body and to the mind. I couldn't get technical about this if I wanted to, but you can ask any doctor in the field and he would accept my basic premise: good, fresh air breathing on a regular basis is essential to best health in mind and body. You destroy this avenue of body-mind improvement and efficiency when you smoke, live in areas of polluted air, subject yourselves to enclosed areas or rooms that are full of other people's smoke, work in areas of high content of gases, fumes, fire smoke, poor ventilation. Strive to breathe clean air deep into the diaphragm, especially when exercising, to maximize your body and mind potential. A byproduct of all this effort is longevity.

Back to the story line. Living into one's eighties by following some of these practices has provided me with the opportunity to examine my values, what I have achieved and failed to achieve, and to seek to change myself for the better. In retirement for well over a decade,

I have relaxed from the formalisms of educational preparations and my professional career paths to mingle with artists in my doodle shows, to stray comfortably away from my lofty academic emeritus pedestal when the spirit moves, to enjoy folks in the music and art worlds, to mingle proudly with and seek knowledge and guidance from spiritually-oriented friends in my church programs. Always a strong believer in my faith, I am now more involved in its activities related to my salvation via two wonderful spiritual and Bible Study courses. I think more about my eternal destiny and wonder what my beloved wife is doing up there in her new Heavenly home. These are issues that I was aware of but was too busy to get involved in, so engrossed was I in my professional work and in traveling for it and in guiding our children along constructive paths. It has all been truly transformational and led me to examining more closely the case for God.

The great appeal to me of God, specifically, is that he holds the answers to every question my intellect wants to ask! He is the solver or explainer of all problems, assuager of all injustices among humankind since the beginning. We live lives of uncertainty, falsehood and half truths—smart about many things, ignorant of many more. Who wants to think of dying with no flattening of mountains of pride and power, arrogance and selfishness; the filling of the valleys of degradation, abject poverty, suffering and ignorance; the making straight of crooked paths of the unrighteous and showing the final destinations of all souls who have practiced good or evil? I look forward to gaining brilliant clarity and, in effect, absolute truth to every doubt or consternation that life and education have generated in the mind about life, the final answers to most of which we will never hear or read as mortals on this planet or explored universe.

Even as I live, I am dying to know, for example, the answers to such questions as to why must there be so much sin and violence and evil in this otherwise beautiful world. Why is there so much punishment of the innocent, especially of the hundreds of millions over the centuries of the children of ignorance, poverty and untimely death? Why do so many vicious or dishonest or undeserving people, many self-absorbed in the pursuit of wealth and self- indulgence—often totally disinterested in God go on to live charmed and seemingly contented lives, while so many essentially good people are punished by miserable diseases or crippled bodies, even painful death? To what temporal or eternal good does such apparent happenstance contribute?

And why this complex panorama of many hundreds of denominations, sects, faiths, beliefs—each housed below their varied steeples—touting different messages and themes about God? Does this represent simply a thriving and beneficial democracy in the elective religious belief field? Or is this indeed the very tower of Babel of Genesis come to life in our time? Every conscience has its choice of refinement or rendition of the Christian or non-Christian message, derived, if it is to classify as Christian, for example, from the life and lessons left to us in scripture by the historical Jesus Christ. As the Bible tells us, by thwarting the ambition to project the tower to reach man's Heaven, God punished the prideful descendents of Sem by inflicting upon them this confusion of tongues. Does not the modern proliferation of tongues reflected in all this smack of prideful individualism and run the risk of straining the patience of God?

Can this multiplicity of interpretations of God's message really serve his divine plan here on earth? Who is to say? I would prefer to believe that it *is* a good thing that the many millions who populate the variety of Christian denominations and sects, as well as the millions more of non-Christian religions around the world, are all under Christ's umbrella, for the majority of them, too, believe in God. In a sense, it is analogous to the wide variety of foods man and woman ingests to sustain and strengthen the human frame. The image of Christ, I like to think, is enriched by the vast number and variety of Christians who believe him to be our Savior, and by the even greater number in our world who, though non-Christian, also believe in God. God himself knows, even if they don't, that it is He they are thinking of, which redounds to his glory.

And if there is a "Who," at what stage in this skein of increasing uncoiling of religious opinion will that "who" convey the ultimate truth about belief to all mankind? Does not the logic in every human mind yearn for answers to these questions? And who but God can provide those answers without challenge? Death itself and alone in the blackness of its futile finality offers only silence and nothing else. In faith, our certitudes are enriched with deep divine mysteries about all this, and yet in those divine mysteries we must find nourishment for faith in God: it is, it is—yes, it *is* our only hope.

In addition to all these questions, there are so many, many others of a personal nature that accumulate in a lifetime that would so tragically all go unanswered if there were no all-knowing God in eternity for us to anticipate. I passionately look forward, for example, to learning on the Day of Judgment who, among all those I knew personally or in or outside of the extended family, as well as who among the rich and famous, got through the Pearly Gates to Paradise, who wound up consigned to purgatorial rehab and who, alas—if any—descended to biblical Gehenna, a place of still worse torment. Or would, indeed, an all-loving God, in any case, send any of his human creatures to suffer eternal fire and brimstone? And, how many of those who committed dastardly crimes on earth and escaped the death penalty because of either astute legal finesse, prosecutorial incompetence or prevailing religious beliefs, also escape God's condemnation on the basis of the Divine's more supremely refined imperatives on innocence, guilt and mercy? Can God's forgiveness always be taken for granted, even if we confess and repent?

On the positive plain about my passion to witness an afterlife, I want desperately to see everyone again—all the people we loved in life who have gone on before: my deceased mother and father, my three brothers and two sisters, especially my beloved twin sister, in childhood my constant chum, who died of diphtheria at the age of eight. I want to see Jennifer and Robin, two innocents of ours who died in childbirth. And should I achieve—however undeservedly it may be—eternal salvation, I would want in God's good time, to greet my own children, their spouses and spouses' families and my grandchildren and their families and connections, when they each and all arrive in the vestibule of Heaven. I hope to see, too, all those many aunts and uncles, cousins, grandparents I had known in youth, as well as those I never met of my saintly mother's parents and relations who never left Ireland. And I am eager to experience definitively, also, the spiritual and physical form in which all these reunions will occur. The wonderful book, *Every Thing You Ever Wanted to Know About Heaven (But Never Dreamed of Asking),"* by Dr. Peter Kreeft, has helped me to visualize in more practical terms what those who have passed on may be experiencing.

I cannot understand why anyone thinking logically and dispassionately about all this could possibly not yearn for such knowing outcomes following our demise from this planet! Everything that occurs in reality among humans on this earth seems to me ineluctably oriented toward this divine denouement.

On the matter of free will, our most prized privilege from God: life without it would make us automatons—robots; it would be weird to say the least, difficult even to imagine. But, ah, the issue of what price we pay for it. Take the divine plan for procreation: a beautifully ecstatic expression of love and caring between committed man and woman. Yet consider the associations that have been attached to deviant sexual practices: incest, rape, abortion, transvestitism, adultery, prostitution, promiscuity, infidelity, child and spousal abuse, pedophilia or ephebophelia—even among those tragic few presumed to be dedicated and consecrated to serving God! Some of these transgressions on the divine have been committed by humans in very high social and/or political or religious status. Even at the least offensive level, it seems obvious that a pagan narcissism and immodesty is rampant in our society. Few escape the sins of the flesh. Aside from the awesome positive outcomes associated with procreation, think, on the other hand, of the veritable avalanche of human misery and disease that has eventuated throughout human history by these practices despite God's purpose to facilitate procreation and the expression of profound love and commitment between man and woman!

So, it seems to me pertinent to seek answers to the mystery and apparent randomness of sex when we reach God's domain. Could there be anybody out there on this earthly plain who would not want ultimate answers to these issues? Personally, I anticipate an absolutely convincing rationale that clears up the muddle in my head on this erratic human function. Almighty God will set me straight! Simply dying and being buried won't.

Oh, there are these and many more questions of life and philosophy and belief I want to get closure on at the ultimate Judgment Court, provided, I repeat, I'm not summarily consigned to perdition myself. In other words, God help me, I may not even get the chance to ask these questions!

True, wise theologians past and present may provide answers or partial answers to many of the questions I pose, even as they still proclaim the mystery of God's purposes. I've done my reading; we simply cannot know all that God knows. Still, basically, I want to know, on a personal basis, if the practices and preparations I have engaged in for a long lifetime, and now with more feeling than ever, that are associated with belief and faith in Christ—the novenas, faithful Mass attendance in whatever town or country I was in, the Stations of the Cross, adorations of the Blessed Sacrament, rosaries, the incessant and voluminous absorbing of Catholic apologetics and literature—have been the right practices and the right faith, as I believe in my mind and heart they are. I want my beliefs to be recognized, confirmed and, well yes, rewarded in some modest fashion, at least, though it is a tenet of my Catholic belief that the beatific vision, if vouchsafed us, will surpass all definition of glory: "no eye has seen, nor ear heard, nor heart of man conceived what God has prepared for those who love him" (1 *Cor.* 2.9). In other words, if we are saved, we need not worry; all questions *will be* answered.

While we— none of us— as a practical matter, may talk like this to each other regarding why we believe in God, is not all this why we want a God to be there when we die? Is it not, beside the desire for Heavenly Bliss, the natural irrepressible craving of the unique mind and intellect of human beings to want really final (not relative) answers to all these questions—and more? I think so. Who can deny it but atheists, who face at the end either nothingness under the earth or—if in these ruminations I were to suspend God's mercy for a moment—one hell of a shock! Even at the level of Aristotle's temporal theme that moral virtue is the mean between extremes, the denial of God's mercy seems irrational. Even so, given the universal embrace intended of Christ's startling redemptive act on the cross for those who come to believe in God and who truly repent—for who knows what happens to the mind in the throes of its transit toward Final Judgment—perhaps our all-merciful God will, after due punishments or periods of retribution in the purgatorial regions, even forgive the recalcitrant but questing secularist. For as the official "Catechism of the Catholic Church" says, "Every man who is ignorant of the Gospel of Christ and of his Church, but seeks the truth and does the will of God in accordance with his understanding of it, can be saved."

In sum, given the danger to one's being midst the hail, lightening and accompanying vicissitudes of this life, I marvel at those who have the untutored audacity or foolhardiness to venture out from under God's umbrella.

In a sense, then, in cultivating these right-hemisphere functions of my brain later in life— in contrast to the more analytical, rational and objective demands of my professional life— I have spent more thought and activity on the visual, intuitive, subjective and spiritual. I have found my own pilgrim's progress toward a more balanced appreciation of life and what comes after it.

It is a process that prevails massively among the millions of the retired in the United States, and wherever retired are present. Suddenly you're out of the regular working environment, a huge segment of one's attention formerly committed to assigned daily work processes disappears from one's life; mental and psychic orientations look to shift daily hours into new interests, preoccupations and even profound philosophical and spiritual searches for satisfactory answers for continuing involvement and happiness.

It is hard to put a particular name on anyone's transformation to a deepened faith. No doubt, much of the above at least describes my journey. Blame, also, the initial impetus on my doodles, Gallery X and the trip to the store to buy those dungarees—a symbol leading to meaningful life changes that impinged and enlarged the scope of my life and future.

As for "My Last Dungarees?" It's a possibility, because I am and have always been very slow in wearing out clothes. On the other hand, the doctors tell me I'm a very healthy man for my age, and if the Gallery X artists start showing up in fetching new jean or dungaree styles, I might just make my way out to J.C. Penney again and see how they fit.

Acknowledgments

I owe a great debt of gratitude to Professor Richard Larschan of the English Department at the University of Massachusetts Dartmouth for his mastery of English— its grammatical foundations, rules of punctuation and overall correctness. Assiduously, he read every line of this memoir and made many helpful suggestions. My thanks, also, to Claudia Grace who early on recommended philosophical themes and orientations that added immeasurably from my standpoint to the substance of the book. My creative, insightful and artistic daughter, Mary, pitched in frequently to make a case for putting something in or leaving something out. She loved the cover design, as I did, and that sealed it for me. Other good friends, neighbors and colleagues volunteered to read the manuscript and provided encouraging commentary.

To Nilsa Garcia-Rey and members of the Board who brilliantly run things at Gallery X, where this journey into dungaree land began, to friends of the Arts for guiding me there to display my doodles, to all my offspring and grandchildren for cheering me on in this endeavor, I convey my love and thanks.

Finally, without the assistance, forbearance and skill of the production and design specialists at AuthorHouse—Amanda Koumoutsos and many more than I could name here—this project would not have been so satisfying in its doing and its outcome.

Printed in the United States
220158BV00001B/21/P